26 Weekends in County Jail

Published by Flare Books
an imprint of Catalyst Books LLC
701 La Chapa Unit B El Paso TX 79912 USA
www.catalystpress.org

ISBN Print: 9781963511451
ISBN Ebook: 9781963511734
Library of Congress Control Number: 2025944411

Distributed worldwide by
Consortium Book Sales & Distribution, a division of Ingram
Phone: 612/746-2600
cbsdinfo@ingramcontent.com
www.cbsd.com

Edited by: Robert Berold & Mindy Stanford
Text design and layout: Liz Gowans
Cover design: Brian Garman
Front and back cover photos: Andrew Petrischev/Unsplash.com

First printing
10 9 8 7 6 5 4 3 2 1

Printed in the United States of America

26 Weekends in County Jail

A Quaker Journal of Resistance

by Joseph Olejak

Contents

Prologue

Sometime in May 1996, I was preparing to write a check to pay my taxes like so many other Americans.

I had always complied with the IRS and never thought about it. But this time was different. I had just watched the now-famous interview on CBS 60 minutes with US Secretary of State Madeleine Albright.

For those who may not know the background: since 1990 the United States had imposed massive sanctions on Iraq to punish Saddam Hussein's regime for invading Kuwait. Iraq was barred from exporting its oil, and from importing many products including medicine, medical equipment and food. And it was Iraq's poorest civilians who suffered, not the regime. According to UNICEF, the deaths of children under five exceeded 200 a day due to the sanctions.

In the interview, journalist Leslie Stahl asked Albright, "We have heard that a half-million children have died. I mean, that's more children than died in Hiroshima... is the price worth it?"

Albright replied, "I think this is a very hard choice, but the price—we think the price is worth it."

I couldn't write the check. So many questions were passing through my mind:

- How can withholding food and medicine from a country by an embargo be a moral act?
- How can punishing everyone who lives in that country for the actions of a dictator be justified?
- As a US citizen, what responsibility do I have in this matter?

- Knowing that 50 percent of all taxes go to the military, can I allow my taxes to support a US-brokered embargo which is causing children to die from disease and starvation?

I wrote a letter to the IRS explaining my decision not to pay taxes.

I wrote to all my elected representatives, including President Clinton. I received increasingly threatening letters of demand from the IRS, none of which even acknowledged my objections. This went on for more than ten years. The IRS response culminated in a letter demanding that I appear in person at the IRS offices in the federal building in Albany, NY. I refused to comply.

In 2009, the IRS raided my office and home, taking all my books, records and digital files. In October 2013, I was summoned to appear in the Northern District of New York Federal Court. I was charged with willful failure to file income tax forms and pay the tax.

After much discussion with my lawyer, I understood that I had to decide if I was going to accept the charges and plead guilty, or if I was going to fight them. I learned that if I fought, and forced the system to go through all the steps to convict me, I should expect to face their wrath and be given the maximum penalty: five years in a federal prison. I had a friend who had done something like this, and he'd got five years. It destroyed his health and completely radicalized him against the US government.

My lawyer also made it clear to me that any legal process involving taking on the federal prosecutor would take months, as well a legal bill for $50,000. The judge and prosecutor, he said, would most likely guarantee my conviction by refusing to hear evidence or testimony, which apparently was their legal right.

I pleaded guilty.

In federal court you don't learn the penalty for your crime until the day of sentencing. Six weeks later, on October 13, I found out my sentence:

- 26 consecutive weekends in the county jail
- probation for 5 years
- 200 hours of community service
- pay to the government $262,000 of taxes, interest and penalties

I was now a felon, and about to lose all the money I had.

On a Friday evening in November of 2013, I entered my local prison, the Columbia County Jail, not knowing what to expect, but ready for whatever came next.

This book is a record of the 26 weekends.

◫

Weekend 1

Today is November 22, 2013. Fifty years ago today, JFK was assassinated.

I pass through the front door of the Columbia County Jail. A giant metallic bolt unlocks the door. I pass through a metal detector and enter a dismal world of institutional green.

I'm asked to enter the holding area. A TV is on. Loud. There's a guard, and me, and an overweight Black man sitting behind bars on a wooden bench watching TV.

The guard asks me a bunch of questions about my name, date of birth, and social security number. He asks what clothes I have and fills out a form listing the details: one belt, one pair of shoes, a pair of pants, T-shirt, shirt, jacket, socks and underwear.

I'm asked to go behind a screen and take my clothes off. One at a time, each article of clothing is searched (for drugs presumably) until I'm standing there naked. The guard tells me, "Lift your sac!" I'm confused for a minute, until I realize he's talking about my testicles. I comply. He tells me, "Turn and spread your butt cheeks!" I blush, first in embarrassment, and then in anger at the violation.

He hands me a pile of clothes and tells me to put them on. They include rubber-soled shoes that are two sizes too small. They pinch my toes and I immediately start worrying about my big toe, which has been a problem for years because of an ingrown toenail. Next, a pair of pants and a shirt with black and white stripes. I'm laughing as I put these clothes on because I cannot believe what a cliché this scene is. The clothes, sheets, and blankets have a disgusting smell of rancid oil.

Ⅲ

I'm led to a conference room to wait for the booking officer. About a half-hour later, I'm met by Officer Wyatt, who comes to collect me and reads me the riot act: "I'm gonna tell you what I told the last guy. I don't care what you did out there, but in here, you're all treated the same. You follow the rules and you'll have no trouble." He seems honest and fair. I follow him to the booking room.

Once there I'm interviewed again, this time on video. I'm given a pamphlet on sexual harassment and asked about my property again. Lots of questions about mental health: Have I had any suicidal thoughts? Have I ever been arrested before? Do I see a mental health professional? Do I take illicit drugs or use alcohol to excess? I tell him I'm a Quaker and I'm here because of my deeply held beliefs about non-violence. He says he didn't think there were any Quakers left and asks me where I attend church. I tell him about the Old Chatham Quaker Meeting and he knows the exact stretch of County 13 I'm talking about. After this exchange, I don't feel so freaked out.

Officer Wyatt enters all my responses into the computer. I'm now a bunch of zeros and ones in a database somewhere. I start imagining that days hence, some statistician may see these numbers and think, *This guy's an outlier.*

My picture is taken. I get a bracelet, with a number and a bar code. I've been tagged like a cow and processed, but not rendered. I'm told to go back to the conference room while they process other prisoners from Greene County.

Another half an hour passes. I'm collected and told to pick up a thin "mattress" rolled up on the floor. We start down the hall. The guard talks to me from behind: "Keep to the right when you walk down the hall—some of the guys that work here are by-the-book." I pay attention.

He unlocks a heavy metal door with a giant oversized key.

It makes a big metallic sound. Cell #4 in Cell Block G is open. I pause a moment before I go in. He waits. The cell is painted puke green. There is a stainless steel toilet, a sink, a metal shelf (a bed—if you can call it that), and a table. I walk through the door. My back is to the guard. I hear the door slam.

On the metal shelf bolted to the wall, I roll out the inch-thin foam pad I've been given, stare at the walls, contemplate the place. I hear voices of other inmates.

"Fuck this!"

"Oh, shit!"

I block the sound out.

About an hour later, the book cart rolls around. I'm very happy for this. I choose three books. *Outliers* by Malcolm Gladwell, a book on Buddha and the Twelve Steps, and Isaac Asimov's *Foundation*. Asimov is dated. I put it down. I save the Buddha for another day. Gladwell's book is great. I read it cover to cover. No, I devour it.

The lights go out at 11 p.m. and with that, the auditory torture of the TV ends. But now I have a new torture: the "bed." Let me call it "the rack." It is a three-feet-by-nine plate of metal welded and bolted to the wall. The rack and the foam pad with its attached "pillow" (a slice of vinyl) constitute my bed.

7:00 a.m. Saturday. The lights and the TV come on. I cover my head with the blanket. My back is killing me; my hip is on fire and I've got pain going all the way down my iliotibial band, that swath of muscle and ligament that runs down the side of your leg from hip to knee.

"Chow time!" an inmate calls out to me, and warns: "You

better get it before it's gone."

Breakfast is Rice Krispies, a banana, white toast, milk and juice. I'm pleasantly surprised by the quality of the coffee. It actually tastes good. As a meal goes, this breakfast is basically processed white carbohydrate plus the banana. Not enough protein and no fiber. Eat this for very long and you'll be heading for diabetes!

An inmate comes for my tray. He counts the cups carefully. I don't have a cup in my cell, or a toothbrush or toothpaste. Prison is a place where you have to ask for everything you need. The Corrections Officer (CO), becomes your lifeline. Hours often transpire between the request and the response. Some COs don't acknowledge the requests or even make eye contact. I wonder about this. Maybe they're worried about being manipulated by inmates into doing something they don't want to do.

It's just before noon. I need to use the bathroom, but now the CO on watch is a woman. I'm concerned about her coming around when I'm on the toilet. I'm suddenly modest. I don't want my personal space violated, least of all by a woman, and I don't want any interaction with her while I'm defecating. I have noticed a rhythm the guards seem to adhere to. They walk around with a little scanner and scan a barcode on the walls of the cell block every half hour on the 15th and 45th minute. I wait for her to come around again and hope I don't shit myself in the meantime.

I spend most of the day reading. I'm grateful to have books and my eyeglasses. When I'm not reading, I try to do yoga on the floor of the cell or just sit in quiet meditation.

At 11 a.m., Dan Michaud and Eric Bear from the Quaker Intentional Village in Canaan (QIV-C) visit me. I'm very happy to see them. We talk about QIV-C and my involvement in the Quaker community. At 11:45 a.m., the guard comes to tell me lunch will be served shortly. I'm escorted back to my cell.

Lunch looks like beef stew on rice, overcooked green beans and broccoli and carrots, milk and apple crumble. In the world of food, it is an acceptable meal. I could actually feel satisfied by this food.

I think of the serenity prayer before I eat:

O God and Heavenly Father,
Grant to us the serenity of mind
to accept that which cannot be changed;
courage to change that which can be changed;
and the wisdom to know the difference.
Through Jesus Christ our Lord, Amen.

I meditate on the phrase "courage to change the things that can be changed and the wisdom to know the difference..." How can you know in advance what, if anything, will come from taking action? The truth is you don't and you can't know. It comes down to a kind of sixth sense. You just feel it. Am I making any difference by sitting inside a jail cell? A memory comes to me of a friend saying: "We don't always see the big picture, but we have to trust that we have a part in its gradual unfolding." I think on that.

2:00 p.m. I retreat into my mind. I push out the noise of the TV.

2:30 p.m. I'm called out to see the nurse for a TB test. At last, the test room is joyfully quiet. I get asked the same questions as before: about thoughts of suicide, drug use, HIV, Hepatitis C, but this time two additional questions: Have I ever had a heart attack / cardiovascular disease? and Do I have any food allergies? She takes my blood pressure. It's 137/85. That's high for me. Usually, my blood pressure is 115/70. I'm sure it is the noise pollution in this place. I'm aware of a 2003 study on the health effects of noise, including nervous system damage.[1]

Apart from the TV's noise, I really don't want its content of sex and violence transmitted to my ears for 18 hours a day.

It's 3:50 p.m. In Cell Block B, cell number 2, I break into tears reading "The Peace Testimony of George Fox" in his *Quaker Journal.* I am not scared or frustrated. I am not angry or sad. I feel deeply connected with what he is saying.

Dinner is at 5:15. Baloney sandwich, milk, pudding. Nothing green. Yuk. The processed meat looks like rubber and is probably full of cancer-causing nitrates. I drink the milk and push the tray under my cell door. My cell neighbor asks if he can eat it. I reply, "I'm not sure you want to eat that, but be my guest."

7:00 p.m. I meditate. I get still. I realize I'm here as a political dissident. I consider how I can make this experience count.

10:30 p.m. I can't stand the noise any longer. I cover my head with a blanket and try to fall asleep on the steel slab.

I'm awake before sunrise. It is quiet. I stand on the bunk and look out the window high above me. It's the golden hour. The light is at an acute angle and there is a golden glow on the razor wire that surrounds the basketball court outside. Four birds fly in the distance. I envy them.

I hear someone shouting. I realize it's me he's shouting at.

"Get off of there! No standing on the bunk."

I know this CO, his name's Whistler. He's six foot three. Imposing. Also loud and arrogant. I don't like him and I have to deal with my own disgust at his behavior.

He walks by my cell and I turn my back. I will not look at him. I overhear a snippet of a conversation he has with another prisoner: "What are you, a retard? Are you gonna be a pain in the ass my whole shift?" I don't know what the inmate has asked or done, but the CO's tone of voice is clearly disrespectful.

Why does he act like this? I conclude he is as much a prisoner as I am. He spends eight hours a day, forty hours a week, fifty weeks a year in this shit hole; a place that offers no creativity, innovation, or self expression. Yes, he may have autonomy over his physical movement, but he has no autonomy over his thinking. His responses are completely predictable. He is a prisoner of his own mind.

The rest of the day moves at a glacial pace. I'm restless.

4:45 p.m. I tell the CO I'm a "weekender" and remind him to release me at 6:00. He tells me they'll get me out.

5:59 p.m. My bed is rolled up. I'm waiting.

6:20 p.m. I'm still waiting. I'm pacing and I'm getting angry. What is going on?

6:25 p.m. A guard comes to take me out. I ask for a phone call. Officer K, the booking CO, apologizes for letting me out late. I begrudgingly accept his apology, but I'm mad.

I change my clothes and stand outside the cage. He passes the phone through a square hole in the wire. I dial. It's ringing and ringing. I'm getting anxious that my daughters are not home, that I've missed them.

Finally, the answering machine picks up.

"You've reached the home of the family Olejak. We are not home. Please leave a message and we'll get back to you as soon as we can... Beep."

"Hi girls, it's Papa. I'm still in Hudson, but I'm on my way to take you out to dinner. See you in 25 minutes. I love you."

As I hand the phone back, I can see the expression on the CO's face. He understands why I'm unhappy, and it has nothing to do with spending an extra 25 minutes in the jail.

Once outside, I run though the cold night air and let out a yawp at the top of my lungs. I'm free again. I feel like I'm five years old. My legs feel like new.

WEEKEND 2

This weekend, as I left home for the jail, I was thinking of the early Quakers. They were so committed to their faith that at times the only ones left to attend meetings were children: all the adults had been jailed for upholding their beliefs.

In my case too, my children have been left behind.

In two ways. First, I am unavailable to parent them when I am locked up. Obviously, 26 weekends is not a terrible sentence compared to the solid five years for federal tax crimes, but it still costs my children. Weekend after weekend, they do not have the emotional and physical presence of their father. What is going through their minds? Where's Dad? Why don't other kids' fathers disappear for half a year of weekends? When you're young, that awkwardness can feel very strange.

The second way is financially. I made it clear from the beginning that I get half my income from motivational talks that I give over certain weekends. In advance of the sentence, my lawyer had given the court and the probation department the dates of these weekends. The judge, in his remarks at sentencing, told me: "You have an ultimate responsibility to raise those two young people in a proper manner and according to your religious convictions" and yet there was no provision in the sentence to allow me particular weekends off to earn the money to fulfill this obligation. Apparently my ultimate duty "to raise those two young people" is overruled by the ultimate need of the federal government to feed its insatiable maw.

Which brings me to the topic of prison food. To call it food is a long shot. It is closer to Processed Un-food Kanned Emptiness (also known as PUKE). I have studied clinical nutrition for over 25 years, and I can tell you that the PUKE served at jail is guaranteed to cause the following:

metabolic syndrome
endocrine dysfunction
cancer
immune breakdown
gut disturbances (from gluten)
constipation (from lack of fiber)
emotional disturbances
abnormal heart function
high blood pressure, and
peripheral vascular damage

These ten conditions are a short list. I'm sure there are plenty of other problems associated with this diet.

Here is what prison food will do to you and why:

- *Processed Un-food Kanned Emptiness is just empty calories:* A prison diet is composed mainly of empty calories that come from high-glycemic-index processed foods from cans or bags, such as Rice Krispies, corn flakes, white bread, Jello, potatoes (cooked or as chips) and pretzels. These kinds of foods create sugar spikes in the blood, followed by insulin spikes, followed by increases in insulin-like growth factor. Elevated blood sugar, and elevated insulin, over time damage blood sugar regulation mechanisms in the body. An insulin-like growth factor has been associated with prostate cancer, bowel cancer and breast cancer. To call this diet deadly is not an exaggeration.
- *Insulin spikes create endocrine dysfunction:* The entire endocrine system is based on a delicate balance between catabolism (breakdown) and anabolism (building up). Insulin is an anabolic hormone (it makes you grow). It stores fat and brings sugar into the cell for use in respiration. When it is secreted in large amounts with daily spikes, it

wreaks havoc on the thyroid and adrenal glands and sets the body up for endocrine dysfunction, not right away, but in months or years.

- *Insulin spikes lead to cancer:* When there is more insulin-like growth factor in circulation, cancer becomes more prevalent.
- *Immunity breakdown arises from refined carbohydrates:* It is a well-researched fact that refined sugar damages white blood cell counts and leukotaxis (the movement of white blood cells): two factors necessary for a properly functioning immune system. Steve, an inmate in my cell block, had shingles: a herpes zoster infection of the nerves usually associated with immune breakdown. It is rarely found in 28-year-olds like him. But without the proper nutrients for immune support, within five months, Steve was experiencing the very painful side effect of shingles: burning pain along a nerve.
- *Chronically high levels of gluten damage not only the gut but also the brain:* Gluten is a causative factor to damage of the gut brush border, the delicate collection of cells and microbes that keep the bad stuff in and let the good stuff through. For those in jail with a history of substance abuse, the prison diet is a catastrophe for their brains and brain chemistry. Given the scientific research, one could even say that the prison diet is criminally negligent on this issue, because it promotes disease. We incarcerate people for poisoning others, don't we? How is the food provided by the prison system any different?
- *Lack of fiber and bowel dysfunction:* There is a clear link between lack of fiber and abnormal bowel function. Fiber also plays a major role in gut flora balance. Recent research shows the pivotal role that gut flora play in neurotransmitter regulation of mood and weight gain.

- *Emotional health requires Omega 3 fats:* The brain is composed mainly from fats derived from Omega 3 in the diet. Numerous studies have shown that low intake of Omega 3 fats affect brain functions, including learning, memory, depression, and anxiety.
- *Abnormal heart function:* Without certain vitamins—especially the B and C complex from whole grains like buckwheat, barley, millet, quinoa, and oats—dysregulation of heart rhythm is just a question of time. The first sign of this is a change in heart rate variability, an independent measure of heart health.
- *High blood pressure:* The prison diet causes vascular damage, a direct result of carbohydrate-induced hyperlipidemia and inflammation.
- *Inflammation:* Intake of calories without nutrition is inflammatory. The prison diet is completely lacking in Omega 3 fats, as well as complex phytonutrients from uncooked plants and a basic balance of macro nutrients. This leads to an increase in inflammatory prostaglandin formation, which is directly tied to vascular disease and cancer.

As with toxic food, there is also the toxic economics of the prison system. Even after one weekend, I saw how the prison system is filled up with people who lack economic opportunity. Government has constructed a complex web of rules, regulations, statutes, and laws that guarantee the prison system a perpetual source of "clients." Those who benefit are not the prisoners but the lawyers, judges, police, and correctional institutions that feed off people like parasites.[2]

It's because the system we have is based on punishment, not restorative justice. A just society looks at the causes of problems and seeks solutions. Punishment alone addresses nothing. The numbers of inmates that return to prison speak for themselves.

The book I'm reading, Malcolm Gladwell's *Outliers*, makes it evident that time, place and social circumstances play a big role not only in whether one succeeds, but also in whether one is able to imagine success.

Only some people in jail are hardcore recalcitrant; most of them are people who have turned to crime because of the socio-economic stratum they were born into. I was deeply impressed with the message of Pope Francis when he spoke on income inequality, as quoted in the *National Catholic Reporter* of 26 November 2013[3]:

> Today everything comes under the laws of competition and the survival of the fittest, where the powerful feed upon the powerless. As a consequence, masses of people find themselves excluded and marginalized: without work, without possibilities, without any means of escape.
>
> Human beings are themselves considered consumer goods to be used and then discarded. We have created a "throw away" culture which is now spreading. It is no longer simply about exploitation and oppression, but something new. Exclusion ultimately has to do with what it means to be a part of the society in which we live; those excluded are no longer society's underside or its fringes or its disenfranchised: they are no longer even a part of it. The excluded are not the "exploited" but the outcasts, the "leftovers."

The solution to crime is not punishment: the solution is fairness and opportunity. Of all the industrialized nations, the US has the highest percentage of its people incarcerated. In 2013, "an estimated 6,899,000 persons were under the supervision of adult correctional systems."[4] There is something very wrong with this picture.

Income inequality is a kind of social crime that is begging for justice. But none can be found, because the people who have the money are buying the politicians and judges who make the rules. What we see over the last 60 years is increasing aggregation of wealth at the top, and less and less at the bottom.[5] For a more detailed look at income distribution in America, see the film *Inequality For All,* a documentary that follows former US Labor Secretary Robert Reich as he looks to raise awareness of the country's widening economic gap.[6]

If you want to know why people are in prison, you don't have to look much farther than this.

◫

One thing that I have not done once in jail is have "a sit-down" (a "number two") on the toilet. I just can't bring myself to do it. It feels so vulnerable. Each cell has one toilet, with no privacy and no door. A female guard could walk in at anytime. Or I'm afraid I'm going to let out some embarrassing sound and be the butt of a joke.

Today one of the guys took a little too long with his "sit down" and was accused by a CO of masturbating on the toilet. This nearly led to an altercation. I almost got pulled into it when Will said, "Hey Doc, I think we found out why his shoulder hurts," as he gesticulated wildly with his right hand. I wasn't going for the bait. If there is one thing I've already learned in jail, it is why people have to put a lid on their anger. It is a pot that is simmering all the time and if just the right remark comes your way, the pot can boil over.

But I was getting uncomfortable around 4:00 p.m., and with two hours to go I was about to make an executive decision on the "number two" situation. Then the urge passed. However, at 5:50, just before my release was due, the urge to purge came back urgent and insistent. I was able to fight it back just long enough to get into the lobby area of the jail where there is a single person privy.

Weekend 3

Juan sold crack. He had spent five years in three different Federal Prisons for that crime. He told me he had been "violated" (jail term for "found to have violated the rules of probation") by his probation officer, for being in contact with his former cellmate. His probation officer asked for his phone records for the past year and when she discovered a phone call that was off limits, he was put back into prison. He's now doing 12 weekends in the county jail for this transgression.

Juan says: "This is the biggest racket they have going. They like to keep you circling in and out and they'll violate you for the smallest thing."

The numbers are bleak for anyone who has interacted with the criminal "justice" system. Christopher Zoukis[7] gives a re-incarceration rate of 76 percent in the US. The criminal justice rules are rigid and inflexible.

Inmates can get their GED or learn a trade while in prison, but the way the system operates is byzantine. In Juan's case, he was one class away from taking a test to obtain his certificate to be a physical trainer when one of the prison guards picked a fight with him. The guard was reprimanded, but Juan was sent to another facility and lost the opportunity to take the test.

In his words: "When you're inside they don't treat you with respect. It's like you are less than human." Juan thinks that because he was about to be released, a guard who didn't like him started the fight on purpose.

I can appreciate his point of view. I've already had some experiences like that myself. When you are first put in a jail, you go into what they call "medical lockup." You are confined to your cell for 23 hours a day—then the nurse is supposed to "clear" you, that is clear you of communicable diseases. On my first weekend, I saw the nurse on a Saturday afternoon and had a TB test, but then I was told that the test could not be read until Tuesday. I didn't want to spend $150 to have the TB test read, so when I returned on my second weekend, I was put back on medical lock up. As soon as I arrived on the Friday, I'd asked to see the nurse so the TB test could be dealt with. The entire weekend went by. The nurse twice entered my cell block, but I was never called out.

I called the facility on Monday when I was home again. The nurse who answered the phone said: "If you're a weekender, it's on you to get yourself cleared." On me? It is my responsibility to manage the medical clearance policy of the Columbia County Jail? I can see why these people do not work in the private sector—they'd be out of business!

Even absurdly small requests, for a book or a pad of paper or a pen, have to go through a convoluted chain of command, even after they had been already approved by the captain of the jail. I asked four different COs five different times for items to be put in my locker and never received them. One CO told me the items were illegal (a book) even though they had been previously approved. Another CO kept putting me off because he was "busy." Busy with what? The place is absurdly overstaffed and there is really not much to do except walk through cell blocks and click on barcodes at opposite ends of the room. The last CO I talked to (a young kid of about twenty-something, who still had his humanity) told me it was up to his supervisor to unlock the locker where my items were kept. His supervisor denied my request. Why? I have no idea. I have been a model prisoner and no trouble to anyone.

The most maddening part of the process is that it appears to be arbitrary and capricious. This one thing makes a person feel out of control, angry and powerless.

I gave up and turned to my yoga practice.

I pulled the pad off of the steel shelf (otherwise known as a bunk) and put it on the floor. I start with a seated meditation. Get quiet. Breathe. Wait on spirit. Fifteen breaths. In and out. The first voice I hear is Paul's from the *Epistle to the Ephesians:* "...the eyes of your understanding being enlightened; that you may know the hope of his calling." I remember why I am in the Columbia County Jail. I was called to this. The spirit of Christ in me.

It feels there are two of me: the earthbound lower self run by fear and survival instinct, and the other higher Self that has been called. The saints talk about the inner battle that goes on inside. I know this inner challenge first hand and I have chosen to listen to Christ's calling.

I move into Child pose. The fascia in my back screams as I stretch my lower back. I breathe through it. Fifteen breaths. I ask for help. *Spirit of Christ in me take this pain away.* Through Child pose to Cat/Dog. Oh, that helps. Breathe in and out. Lying prostrate now I am in Cobra pose. Elbows first, then pushing up onto my hands fully extended. Into Lunge, being mindful to take care of my lower back. Breathing into each pose. Christ at Emmaus enters my mind. I remember how he revealed himself to the travelers on the road. How the spirit of Christ can appear at any time. I open myself up to the spirit of Christ. Welcome the Peace of Christ in me.

Now standing, I'm in Mountain pose. I root myself to the Earth then reach my branches to the sky. Arms up and open, I close my eyes and see a bright blue sky with clouds drifting overhead through the cement ceiling. I feel my inner freedom now. Walls fall away.

I recall the words of my friend and seminar leader Margot: "There is no loss of freedom where you are." This is the experience.

A metal door slams. I am snapped out of my ecstasy. I have to return to myself. This is the practice. Now! Now! Now!

Pete is 18 years old. He got in a fight on 3rd Street in Hudson. He's been charged with assault, larceny and robbery, and now facing 13 years in jail. He's Black, with so little life experience. He's going to be screwed by the system. The public defender has met with him once and is already working out a plea bargain. He has no money for bail, no money for a lawyer, and no knowledge of the law. He does not even understand what the law requires to prove he's guilty of a crime: motive, evidence, and opportunity. His innocence will never get discussed because his guilt is assumed. He's poor, he's Black, and he's not book smart. And he's scared. Scared of the worst. Thirteen years. He'll take five because he knows he's going to get railroaded in a trial. All he has is street smarts. This kid has no chance.

Pete told me he wants to be a nurse. I look at his eyes. They are furtive. "Did you fight that guy?" ... "Did you steal his wallet?" He looks down, says "yes" to the fight, but looks me in the eye and says "no" to the theft. My sense is he's telling the truth. "Where is the wallet?" He says he doesn't know. I think he'd make a good nurse. I see compassion in his eyes. I feel very sad for him.

I want to help this kid.

It's 5:15. Baloney sandwiches again. I can't eat them. I fast on water. My stomach grumbles. In 45 minutes, I'll be out and buy an organic apple.

At the door before the bolt releases with its loud metal clank, I turn to Juan who is also leaving. I ask him, "What's the first thing you're going to do once you're out of here?" He smiles and says, "Kiss my kids."

The door opens—I turn to him and say, "I think I'll do the

same," and run across the lawn to my car. Ice crystals of snow get into my Crocs and tickle my sockless feet. I am alive and thankful for being alive.

Weekend 4

Because the jail nurse has still not cleared me for TB, I have so far been spending the weekends in cell block B, which is the sick bay. But this weekend, I was put in cell block D because there were four guys in cell block B with shingles.

Shingles is a nasty viral infection of the nerve roots that erupts in painful blisters on the skin along the length of a nerve. The pain is excruciating. At mealtime, I noticed one guy had the blisters on his face. I'm fairly certain it was cranial nerve V because his eye did not seem to be affected. He seemed very miserable, which would make sense because the fifth cranial nerve is mostly a sensory nerve. He looked like hell.

I've just realized that I haven't seen the prison cells or any other areas disinfected with anything. Who knows what is lurking on their surfaces? The idea makes my skin crawl. I've taken to washing my hands after touching anything other than my book, even though I know that shingles can only be contracted from a person with an active infection and an open sore.

I have always supported my immune system with herbs (mostly Echinacea root), but as of this weekend, I am going to give myself a loading dose of three herbs to ramp up my white blood cells before each jail visit—Echinacea, Ganoderma & Shitake mushrooms, and Andrographis. I will continue to use them as an insurance policy against infection while I'm in the Columbia County Jail. The COs don't seem to have any idea about infection control policy—the doctor comes in only once a week, and the nurses only dole out meds.

I was seen by the doctor this past weekend and given a cursory exam. He asked about "rods" in my back. These would be Herrington Rods that stabilize the vertebral joints after spine surgery, which would set off the magnetometer they use here for discovering guns and knives. Then he listened to my chest with a stethoscope, and looked in my mouth: checking (I'm guessing) for signs of TB or Strep infection. He did not once make eye contact with me, although his demeanor was polite. I told him that I was kicked by a horse in the back when I was sixteen and had an acquired scoliosis from that injury. He did not make note of it and he did not examine my spine, even though I told him I'd been having back pain.

They all seem to think the same when it comes to pain: "Too bad, buster, this is only a one-star hotel."

For all these reasons, I never take a shower while I am in jail. With six or eight people using the same shower in a day, I worry about fungal infections. The inmates clean the shower once per day by spraying it with a pink fluid. I have no idea what this product contains and whether or not it is anti-bacterial or anti-fungal. No scrubbing takes place on any of the surfaces so I doubt it is clean. Again, my skin crawls when I think about it.

My dear friend Peter Miles was kind enough to mail me a book, *The Immortal Life of Henrietta Lacks*. This amazing story by Rebecca Skloot is about the HeLa cell line that was taken from Henrietta Lacks in the 1950s without her knowledge or consent. What amazes me is the wealth that was generated from a single cache of cells and no one ever considered offering this poor Black woman or her family a nickel. The law is the same today as it was in 1951: once a cell leaves your body, you are no longer the owner and any scientist can manipulate your DNA or cells as they wish and you have no recourse.

One MD is quoted in the book as saying: "It's not like someone in extreme pain with appendicitis is going to negotiate with the hospital about what's going to happen with their tissues after surgery." I was appalled by the arrogance implied in this statement.

We really need some laws with respect to medical research and who gets to profit.

Ⅲ

Weekend 4 has gone very quickly. The only problem was being placed in a cell with a crack in the window caulk. The temperature this weekend was 15 degrees F, and cold air was pouring over my body. I asked for another blanket and thankfully received one, but could not get the chill out of my bones. On Saturday I asked to be moved and this too was allowed. I moved from Cell 4 to Cell 5. Having no draft on me was a major improvement.

In Cell 5, I managed to wrap myself in blankets and with some yoga I was able to raise my core temperature. Thank God for yoga. I choose as my theme for yoga meditation the four agreements:

1. Be impeccable with your word.
2. Don't take anything personally.
3. Don't make assumptions.
4. Always do your best.

With each pose and each breath, I recite these thoughts to myself. In my ending meditation, I recall the words given to me by my friend Jack Allison:

"I am a child of God and I deserve love for no reason."

"I forgive myself for ever forgetting that I am an innocent being of love and light."

An hour in yoga meditation warms me up and refreshes my spirit. I feel good.

The sun sets. The lights outside come on. It is 5:15 p.m. and dinner is served. I pass mine on to the others. The guard comes. I collect my things and take the short walk to freedom.

Cold air fills my lungs. I will see my girls tonight. I'm feeling happy now. I turn on the radio and one of my favorite songs comes on: *Home* by Phillip Phillips. In just a few minutes, I'll have my arms around Manon and Rhéa.

WEEKEND 5

Whistler was the CO intake officer this weekend. As usual, he made degrading comments to all of us as we entered the jail and changed into prison attire.

"Olejak, you old fart, are you in 4?" I don't answer. In my mind, I'm thinking: *He can walk his stupid mouth down here and have a look for himself.* When he actually says something sensible, I will talk with him.

"Juan, you're up. Everything off except your birthday suit. What size you take?"

Juan answers, "Large."

"Large? Are you kidding? That's not what the girls tell me!"

Long pause. Juan responds: "Oh man, don't insult me like that."

Juan is standing there naked, waiting for his clothes. Whistler says: "By the looks of things down there, I'd say you're more like a small."

The jail has a very explicit policy against sexual harassment. Whistler thinks he'll remain anonymous and that inside the green cement-block walls, he's the law. What he doesn't know is that I'm a scribe.

As I wait my turn for prison clothes, I recall a verse from Proverbs: "Smart people speak wisely... but the foolish talk too much and are ruined."

I'm a little worried about what kind of trash talk is going to happen when it's my turn. I just happen to be wearing a pair of boxers I received from my nine-year-old daughter for Christmas two years ago. They are powder blue with a picture of Frosty the Snowman. Definitely not macho.

Whistler, not satisfied with degrading Juan, starts on the guy in cell 2: a kid who looks about 19. He got 30 days for disorderly conduct; a fight or something. He's unshaven, but he doesn't have enough scruff to actually make a beard.

Whistler: "Hey kid, you have foot in mouth disease or something? These shoes smell like a cat box!"

"I paid $150 for those Jordans."

Whistler retorts: "Well, you paid about $100 too much, dude. And those powder blue shorts and T-shirt are gay—why don't you get some real clothes?"

"What! Like black?"

It is clearly a mistake to smartass Whistler back. He's dressed in a black Sheriff's department uniform so he does not appreciate this remark. He makes the kid stand there naked taking his time looking for shoes, a T-shirt, pants, etc.

The message is loud and clear: Shut the fuck up. However disrespected you feel, you will be subjected to the power differential.

I'm the last one up. I strip down, but I leave my cross and New Testament on the counter where it is clearly visible. I'm making my own statement, which is something like: "I'm operating from a different place than you are."

We only exchange a few words about clothes size and about a piece of tape inside the Bible (apparently a concern over contraband). My boxer shorts are never mentioned. I feel the power of His presence and am thankful. In a minute or two, I'm changed and out of there.

◫

I'm now in Cell Block G. For the first time I will not be locked in my cell for twenty-four hours. My TB test came back negative and I was cleared to be in the "gen pop" (short for "general population"), meaning I am with other inmates sharing the common living areas and routines. This is a boon for socializing, but not for reading. Deepak Chopra will have to wait.

Jack is the "Mayor" of Block G. After I was locked in on Friday night, he came right over and struck up a conversation. Jack knows everything there is to know about this place: all the guards, and who are the jerks and who are "okay." He'd say things like: "There goes CO Blake —he's not bad but he's by-the-book," and "Watch out for Sarge. We call him Dinosaurus because he's like a Tyrannosaurus Rex when he gets mad."

"Oh?" I reply.

"Yeah, Sarge's brother blew his head off or something and he's got a little anger issue."

Right then and there, I decide I'm not going to have any interactions with Sarge.

Jack relates a situation that happened before I got to the jail in which there was some contraband found (cigarettes and marijuana cigarettes) and Dinosaurus "tossed" all the cells and threw everything all over the place looking for stuff.

Jack says: "It's amazing what you can get away with in here if you know how." I don't want to know anything about how to traffic in contraband and quickly change the subject.

CO Padgett enters G Block and does his half-hourly rounds. He casts a suspicious glance at Jack, who blurts out: "WHAT?" Padgett says: "You know what."

I learn a day or two later that the cell tossing that went on was related to Jack getting caught with cigarettes. He spent 140 days in 24-hour lock up because of that.

"You see that ventilation shaft?" Jack points up to the ceiling and the two grates above the toilet. I know he's going to tell me something I don't want to hear. "One grate is hot air in ... the other is the cold return. If you want to smoke and not get caught, all you have to do is wait for the system to come on and blow your smoke into the cold return vent... it works every time."

"Except that time you got caught," I say.

He laughs: "That wasn't my fault. The trusties ratted me out."

I'm so naïve. "Trusties?"

"Yeah, trusties are the guys who work in the kitchen and get special favors from the guards. All you have to do is be willing to snitch on someone."

I'm beginning to see that this is not a place where it is easy to trust people. Not that I have anything to hide, but there is always the problem of not knowing what you don't know. The blind spot. I take a secret vow to keep my eyes and ears open and my mouth shut. I clearly have a lot to learn now that I'm gen pop.

◫

Sully was in the Columbia County Jail on a drug charge. The police found 15 empty bags in his truck and 4 containing dope. Sully said the dope was for personal use. The DA charged him with trafficking in cocaine. It is very hard to know what to believe. I look in the eyes. Sully's eyes dart from the ground up to my eyes. I have the sense I'm getting half-truths from him, but I can't be sure. Oddly, I like this kid.

We talk and walk in circles as we enjoy the 55-degree air. The sky is grey and overcast with the heaviness of moisture in the air. It feels like it's going to rain any minute, but I don't care. I'm happy to be outside the stuffy confines of G block.

I'm shocked to learn from Sully that the Columbia County Jail spends about three dollars per day per prisoner on food. Sully worked in the kitchen as a trusty, and informs me that most of the food is canned and arrives on a truck from Ginsberg Food Distributors. The jail has full kitchen facilities, but there is very little actual cooking going on. When Sully was jailed previously (about three years ago), he said the food was much healthier and there were decent portions so you don't always feel hungry.

I ask Sully about his interests. He says he likes *Popular Science* and *Popular Mechanics*. "I can build just about anything," he says. I ask how he got mixed up in all of this and Sully recounts his story: getting hooked on hydrocodone after an injury, then his prescription running out, and the pain persisting. Like so many patients I dealt with as a chiropractor, I revisit the tale of bad medicine when it comes to musculoskeletal injury. Patients are given lots of meds and not very much bodywork for restoring biomechanics.

I can feel the anger rising up in me. I realize that if this kid had gotten the right treatment, he would probably not be in jail on a drug charge. He is a victim of the pharmaceutical system—treat symptoms, push drugs, ignore causes, and when the shit hits the fan, let the penal system take over.

▥

The recreation yard is voluntarily segregated. Jack says: "Don't go over there—that's A Block—the murderers and pedophiles. See that old guy right there? He sexually assaulted a 13-year-old girl. If that had been my kid, I'd feed him his heart after I ripped it out of his chest."

I feel very sad just then. Sad for the girl who was sexually violated, but also sad for this 65-year-old guy. He is in hell. A pariah among criminals, and he looks so frail as he walks. He's got that characteristic walk old people get when they're not sure where their feet are landing and each step is a kind of step-and-lurch. I can't bring myself to look into his eyes as we pass. I think of my own daughter being in the full bloom of youth and the promise of life ahead of her. Yet I feel compassion for him too, and am ashamed of it. I should hate him, but I can't really bring myself to do it.

▥

Dominoes. The "mayor" organized the game. It is me and the mayor against the two Carls—two guys both named Carl whose last names I can't recall. I have no clue how to play dominoes and I keep making the mistake of watching my hand, as if I'm looking for a straight flush or something, instead of counting the playing pieces and finding a way to shut down our opponents.

"Chuchatsu!" Ugh! We've lost again because of me. Chuchatsu is when a player goes out playing his last domino and locks up the board, at the same time preventing other players from playing their bones. I think the mayor made up the term because I can't find it anywhere. I'm embarrassed, but these guys are cutting me a lot of slack because I've been answering their medical questions all afternoon.

Once you laugh with people over a game, trust develops and stories appear. Carl #1 tells us about having kidney stones in jail. "They refused to take me to the hospital and I was in agony, puking in my cell because I was in so much pain." I asked if they'd offered any pain medication. Carl said yes but he'd refused it because he'd been diagnosed with rheumatoid arthritis as a child. He told me he'd taken so much Ibuprofen, he didn't feel good on it any more. "They just gave me gallons of tea and told me to drink as much as I could. It hurt like hell to pee."

Carl probably has no idea of the damage non-steroidal anti-inflammatory drugs have on the kidneys and that his kidney stone may even be due to lowered kidney function from years of Ibuprofen or Acetaminophen use. I glance down at his hands for the first time. His knuckles are enlarged at the end of his fingers. I can see the early signs of joint damage. This kid has already had a hard life.

It's about 85 degrees in G Block. Outside it is 60 degrees and the heat is still on. Carl #1 is mixing up the dominoes with his shirt off. A multi-color tattoo on his shoulder reads in elaborate script "Love Conquers All."

"What's that?" I ask pointing to the tattoo.

"Oh that's for my kid who died of SIDS."

My heart sinks.

The other Carl (he's 19 and hasn't mastered impulse control) blurts out: "What the fuck is that?"

I give Carl #2 the evil eye and explain that SIDS stands for Sudden Infant Death Syndrome. Doctors still don't fully understand why it happens, though there is some speculation that it may be due to birth trauma to the highest parts of the spinal cord.

Now he's got all kinds of questions, but Jack has the good sense to shut him down. Carl #1 with the tattoo is sitting there, head bowed and sullen. Then he says: "We didn't want to get pregnant—my girlfriend and I—but once I found out she was pregnant, I wanted the baby." His voice trails off to a faraway place.

Carl #2 is 23. He's disabled because of the damage the rheumatoid arthritis did to the synovial joints in his lower back. I can see it in his posture and the way he walks. I'm sure the horrible sleeping conditions in this place are no help to him. He asks me for a chiropractic adjustment, but I can't. I'm worried about hurting him without first getting an MRI to see what is going on. If I did that, I could lose my license. I can see the headline: *Chiropractor Loses License after Paralyzing Inmate without Proper Diagnostic Work-Up.*

But I have another idea: yoga in G Block. Since the publication of a news article on my Quaker War Resistance stance, it became well known in the jail that I was a chiropractor. I had to fend off requests for treatment, but felt bad because I wanted to help the inmates, so many have chronic back pain.

Late on Sunday afternoon, I take the one-inch-thick foam pad from my cell, place it on the floor in the middle of G Block, and start doing yoga. In a few minutes, the two Carls and Jack and Stuart are looking down on me.

I'm on my knees in Child pose stretching my lower back fascia and Carl #2, ever the wise-ass, blurts out: "Are you a fucking Muslim?"

I point to the opposite wall—"Mecca is that way. No, this is yoga, and this posture is called Child pose—it's good for your lower back." In no time, there are four mats on the floor and the new CO, a woman, comes into the block and says, "What the hell is this?"

Carl #2 blurts again: "Yoga!"

I'm smiling on the inside.

"Okay, guys, the whole trick to this is to breathe once you get into the posture. Fifteen deep breaths. Let your spine relax into it. Focus on the in and the out of your breathing."

I go through five poses (Lunge, Cat/Dog, Cobra, Child and Corpse). When we get to the end, I say: "If you have a mantra, a good thought or prayer to focus on, you can think about it here when you're just lying flat and relaxing. Mine is 'I attract all things good and beautiful toward me'."

Carl #2 laughs.

I say, "You can make up whatever you want, just keep it short and positive."

The CO, who's been observing all this with a smirk on her face, orders me up.

"Olejak—You're out of here. Pack up your stuff."

As I head toward the door, these four guys whom I've gotten to know over the last forty-eight hours each give me a fist bump to say, "You're alright."

I take it in and say, "Merry Christmas."

WEEKEND 6

Whistler is the booking CO again. I'm ready for him this time. Black T-shirt and black underwear. Much to my surprise, he does not insult any of us. We are in and out of the changing area in a jiffy. Maybe he's not the jerk I think he is.

Then I realize that I'm guilty of cutting down his humanity to the extent that I feel he has cut down my own. I don't feel very charitable about thinking bad thoughts about Whistler. A twinge of guilt sweeps momentarily over me. When he hands me the books out of my locker, I look him in the eye for the first time—a dignity I had withheld from him, and from myself.

This weekend, I was thrust unexpectedly into gen pop—in a place called D-Dorm. Six bunk beds. Eleven guys. A shower. A toilet. Two steel tables.

I really wanted to have some privacy this time because, as the weekend was approaching, I came down with a mild case of the flu. After hammering down a half bottle of Andrographis, Echinacea, Ganoderma/Shitake and whole Desiccated Spleen, I was feeling okay by Friday, but tired and weak. I just wanted peace.

I should have known there'd be none of that. It seems that whatever you want in jail they give you the exact opposite.

Getting to sleep is never easy in jail, because not only do you get the TV jocks commenting on the fight, you also hear things like, "Elbow him in the face, motherfucker" and "Dropkick his ass, dude" from the commentators. Periodically, fights break out just because of a difference of opinion on a referee call.

I was fortunate enough to have a top bunk, about two feet away from the garish light and incessant buzz of a fluorescent fixture. At 8:00 p.m., two hours after my arrival, I could not keep my eyes open any longer. I wrapped myself in blankets like a mummy to block out the lights above my head and the noise of the TV, now tuned to kickboxing.

Finally, the bliss of sleep overtook the assault on my ears. I slept for the next eleven hours.

Waking up on the metal rack was no picnic. My ear felt like a head of cauliflower, but that wasn't quite as bad as my lower back. The skin over my sacrum felt raw and the numbness was down my left leg into my calf. I was hoping this was temporary—a circulation thing—and that I was not going to have another week of agony.

"You crashed out pretty early last night," said Sully.

Sully's a guy who has been in and out of jail on heroin charges.

"Yeah, I think I needed to sleep off some remaining flu—I felt like crap when I got here." Without elaborating to Sully, I think the stress of the holidays and being in and out of jail is starting to get to me.

I get down and walk about a little. I felt like the ten-thousand-year-old man initially, but thank God, the numbness subsided once the circulation returned.

After cornflakes, coffee, and milk with toasted white bread, the books I had ordered thankfully arrived. *Wild* by Cheryl Strayed and *Proof of Heaven* by Eban Alexander, MD.

I delved into Strayed's book straight away. Having some familiarity both with the death of a mother from cancer and the Appalachian Trail (the sister trail to the Pacific Coast Trail on the eastern seaboard), I wanted to know about this author's experience. Reading her vivid passages about nature and emotional scars reminded me of how important it is to be in the silence nature provides, and its access to the soul. This is a part of myself that I have neglected in recent years.

The last time I hiked a section of the Appalachian Trail was back in my early twenties. I remembered doing a day hike to Bear Rock Falls from Mt. Everett State Park, rappelling down the face, then climbing up the face. That was far too long ago.

Ⅲ

Within a few chapters of *Wild,* I was contemplating my own life path. I wanted to flip to the back of Cheryl Strayed's book to see if it was going to have a happy ending. In case you haven't read it, I won't tell. But I am not so sure about me. The path forward looks absurdly steep.

My mind drifts back to the time I climbed the Dent de Midi in Switzerland. It's 9,000 feet of trail that ends in a trek up a glacier. When you get to the top, you can't do more than focus on one footfall at a time unless you've trained for it. At the time I did the Dent de Midi, I was in my mid-thirties. My hiking companion was a 60-year-old Swiss man who laughed at my slow pace. I made it, but it was a slog.

I'm not so sure about the path before me now. I've only done six weekends of the twenty-six and I already fantasize about getting lost on the Pacific Coast Trail or the Appalachian Trail.

With each chapter of *Wild*, I pack my bags to a different destination. So far, I've chased the high peaks of the Andes to Lake Titicaca on a motorcycle, the narrow valleys of Northern Italy on small gauge railways, and the barren lavender places of the Scottish highlands. All sound much better than the puke green walls of the Columbia County Jail. The hardness of every surface and the violence on the eyes and ears is tough. No escape from the assault on the senses here. The boredom is intense too, even though I try to protect my mind with good books and keen observation of my surroundings.

Have the last six weekends changed my mind any about my deeply held beliefs? I'd have to say no. The stupidity of government on so many levels looks as idiotic as ever. I am more committed than ever to a compassionate world that works for everyone.

In education, we have metrics for success; points for completing assignments, finishing labs, attendance, etc. If you work hard and study and apply yourself, you can be a valedictorian or salutatorian. You may be rewarded with a scholarship. At every turn, a student faces the consequences of skipping class, cheating, and missing exams. But if you are the government, you can fuck up in the worst ways. The kinds of ways that ruin people's lives or ruin entire countries, and for which there are no consequences. Presidents, Congress, judges, cops, and prosecutors are all immune from the kind of oversight and scrutiny that attaches so acutely to everyone else.

The system demands respect but not because it is deserved. It demands respect in the way a raging bull deserves respect: it will kill you if you can't find a way out of its path.

What is the way out? Is poverty, or simplicity, a way off the merry-go-round? Expect less, want less, earn less. Focus on a few things that matter? I don't know.

◫

On Saturday, the guys were kind enough to leave me alone until after lunch, but I could tell there was a backlog of questions about that article on me in the newspaper. Not so much about being a Quaker (although there were some questions about if Quakers really still existed), but about being a chiropractor. I got one request after another along the line of: "My back is killing me, can you help me, Doc?"

The problem of chronic back pain is everywhere in this wretched place. These inmates don't get any treatment or advice on what to do about their back pain—they just live with it. The position of the Columbia County Jail and its medical staff can be summed up as: "We will provide the bare minimum of care. Unless you are dying, you will not go to a hospital or see any other medical professional. End of story."

For people with back pain, the treatment is so far below any proper standard of care that you'd have go to a very run down third world country to see worse. The jail doctor did my "physical exam" (in quotes because looking in the mouth and auscultating the lungs does not constitute a physical exam). His only concern was whether I'd had rods inserted in my back. Without the Herrington rods, about the best you can hope for is Ibuprofen or Acetaminophen: both will create kidney and liver damage when used as directed, even for a short length of time like two weeks.

I asked about a better sleeping pad for my cell and was flatly turned down.

So are we talking about a little discomfort from a bad bed? Am I and the 140 other inmates just supposed to toughen up and quit being wimps? Not quite. What I saw in D-Dorm was everything from chronic headaches due to neck pain (the pillows are completely inadequate to support the neck while sleeping) to scoliosis and sciatic neuritis (pain down the leg) as well as other lesser known nerve syndromes of the arms and legs. These problems would be taken seriously anywhere else because they could be indicative of any number of conditions, ranging from abnormal alignment of the spine to a herniated disc or an indication of diabetic neuropathy.

For some of these guys, having someone in the jail with them who could actually take a health history, dig for chronicity, and listen to what was going on from a place of concern instead of "what is the minimum I have to do for this guy" was like hitting the lotto.

Jacob was lying in the lower bunk next to mine in the middle of D-Dorm. He spent most of his time in bed on his side because his back was in such pain. He told me he had had scoliosis and the last joint in his spine hurt so bad he could only stand for short periods. Lying on his side with his knees up in the fetal position was the least painful posture for him. One day I was reading my book and I heard what sounded like a whisper: "Hey Doc, do you think you can help me?"

I looked down and saw his face. The most remarkable thing I can remember about it was the crease on his forehead. The kind you get from knitting your brow together, the kind of wrinkle that most people acquire by the time they're 50, after years of pain and frustration. Jacob was 22.

I could not refuse him, but I had to refuse. I needed some time to think my way out of the problem of my own professional standards.

"Let me think about it," I said. "Let's talk after lunch."

Lunch was served. A delightfully tasteless chili over rice with apple sauce, pudding, and milk. "Does anyone have salt?" I said. "This has no taste at all."

Anton piped up: "I've got chicken seasoning." It was in a little plastic pouch and looked like a combination of spices, but tasted like colored MSG. I never eat MSG, but I was desperate. "Mind if I try some?"

"Sure, knock yourself out." This was an act of generosity.

Everything that inmates can get in jail is either paid for through an over-priced commissary or brought in as contraband. And yes, salt is contraband unless you buy it through the jail commissary system, a system that operates as a profit center for the jail. The other is the telephone. Local calls run $1.50 per minute, in a day and age where I can buy a calling card and call Europe for less than five cents per minute.

I decided the only way to treat Jacob and keep myself out of trouble was to draw up an Informed Consent form. Here is what it said:

- I ask that Dr Olejak examine my spine.
- I ask that Dr Olejak provide spinal manipulation to alleviate the pain in my back.
- I realize that Dr Olejak does not have access to diagnostic tests such as CT, MRI or X-ray in the jail.
- I give permission to Dr Olejak to perform spinal manipulation and that if any undiagnosed health issue missed by lack of diagnostic tests results in a problem, I agree to hold Dr Olejak harmless.

I had Jacob sign and date it and then set about explaining where I thought the problem was and what some of the potential things were that could be causing it. Disc damage was one, slippage of one vertebrae on another (spondylolithesis), space-taking lesions, and the like. I told him that at age 22, with a scoliosis and a history of a minor car accident, the problem was most likely due to a lack of motion in parts of his lower back that he could not loosen up himself. Jacob had the habit of twisting his lower back in bed while letting his leg hang off the bed until he got snap. The problem with this, I explained, is that he was only loosening up the parts that were already capable of moving, but doing nothing for the parts of the spine that were severely restricted and causing the pain. "Think of a rusted bike chain," I said. "Which parts need the grease? The links that are moving or the ones that are not?"

Given what I'd told him about the potential risks and

benefits, he wanted to proceed. I examined his spine and located a restriction in his left sacroiliac joint and found that on hip flexion, it was 50 percent less compared to the right side. This could account for his lower back pain. He wanted me to manipulate it back to normal movement, and I did.

I have no idea if I broke any jail rules, but I do know that I'm a licensed chiropractor, that I explained the risks and benefits in an informed consent document, and that I completed a physical exam that included manual orthopedic, range of motion, and some neurological tests to rule out other problems. I'd done my due diligence and I had the patient's permission through all of it. I could not be accused of malpractice or assault. I'd followed the exact same protocol I would have in my office, except for an x-ray and other diagnostic technology.

Jacob stood up and said: "The worst of that pain is gone." And a smile came across his face. And that's when the others started forming a line.

It was then that I looked up and saw Whistler looking through the plexiglass.

"Oh shit!" I thought to myself.

Whistler points to me: "Olejak!"

And then he smiles. "I didn't see that." Definitely not a jerk.

⊞

I ask Sully about the track marks on his arm. Specifically, I want to know why they are on his bicep instead of at the crease in his elbow where the vein is.

"It's better if people don't see the track marks," he says.

"What is it like shooting heroin?" I ask.

"It's the best feeling you'll ever have, but after the first or second time, it's like trying to catch a butterfly on a windy day. That great first high gets harder and harder to find."

"Because you develop a tolerance?"

"Yeah." He looks down and nods his head. I can see that he is trying to remember his halcyon days of heroin before he needed bigger and more expensive doses to get the same effect.

"Tell me about the mechanics of getting high on heroin? How does it work?"

"Well, you can smoke it or shoot it. I smoked it for a while and vowed I'd never shoot it, but one day I was with some people who were shooting and thought how bad can it be to try it once?"

"And? ... How bad was it?"

"Bad? Well, just the first time. I had some nausea, then it was good. Too good. It was the smoothest and best high I've ever had. I didn't care about anything. I had no pain. No worries. Then there was no going back."

What Sully was describing was his neurons adapting to heroin. Heroin affects cells called opioid receptors which are widely distributed in the brain, spinal cord, and digestive tract. They are there because our bodies produce endogenous (made by the body) opiate-like substances, such as endorphins, enkephalins, and dynorphin. The compounds act as neurotransmitters, which are signaling compounds that fit the lock and key of the opioid receptor perfectly. Heroin is not a perfect fit. In fact, because it is a fraction of the endorphin molecule, it stays in the lock for hours, preventing the natural opioids from getting in. The span of the high is how long it takes for this competitive binding of the receptor to unlock. Some scientists think that while heroin occupies the lock, it changes the shape of the lock just enough so that the body starts adapting to heroin preferentially over its own endogenous opioids. This may be one explanation why there is such a high recidivism rate among addicts. Their brains have changed.

I kept inquiring. "Have you ever gone cold turkey?"

"I've gotten short on money a few times and didn't have the cash to buy it. You get this feeling in your stomach that is vaguely uncomfortable as the high wears off. You know you've got maybe two hours to get yourself sorted out or you're going to feel like shit."

"Like shit?" I had a vague idea what withdrawal was like, but I wanted to hear a first-hand account.

"Your stomach hurts. You want to puke. One time I puked like twelve times in a row and this awful green stuff came up. Bile, I think. Trust me—it is the last thing you want to go through. If I had money, I'd always buy enough to make sure I never had to deal with withdrawal."

"But that's a problem, right? Because you don't want to get caught with too much heroin. The more you have on you, the greater the penalty."

Sully lets out a nervous chuckle: "Ah, that's what I'm dealing with right now. I had three or four grams on me when I got caught, but lots of empty bags. They accused me of being a dealer and it was just stuff I'd used over the last few weeks."

I drifted as Sully was recounting his story. I'd heard it before when he was talking to other inmates, but I was interested in what happens when a heroin addict runs out of cash.

"Have you ever run out of heroin? Or the money to buy it? What did you do then?"

"Well, friends of mine have stolen things to get the cash, but that's something I'd rather not do."

"Really, like stolen what?"

"Well, there was this one time when I was really desperate and I broke into an abandoned building with two guys I was shooting heroin with. We cut out the copper with the idea of selling it."

"What was that like?"

"I wanted to cut the copper and put it in bags and hump it down a ravine then bring the truck to pick it up out of sight, but my friends were lazy and insisted on bringing the truck right up to the back of the building. A security guard saw the lights when we were putting the copper in the truck. I threw my tools in the back and dived into the pick-up and we sped off."

"Did you get caught?"

"It wasn't long before the cops were speeding toward the building. Like idiots, we were speeding in the other direction, or maybe the security guard relayed the make of the truck. Anyway it turned into a high-speed chase, but it was futile. We didn't get far."

"How'd that turn out?"

"I did five years upstate."

I talked to Sully a little more about his experiences: "Now that you've detoxed off heroin here inside the jail, do you think it will affect you the same way? Do you think you could walk away from it?"

"I'll never have the same high like that first time, but it'll only take one hit and my body will crave it just like before."

The pleasure center of the brain also takes notice. It's an area called the Nucleus Accumbens. This is the place where we are rewarded for things that feel good. Most people think about chocolate and sex. A heroin user thinks about their next fix.

The first hit of heroin and the rush that comes with it is from a metabolite of heroin called 6-MAM (6-monoacetyl morphine). Heroin is quickly converted in the blood to 6-MAM and, when it crosses the blood-brain-barrier, it binds to µ-receptors (pronounced *mu-* or *mew*-receptors). As you use heroin, more and more of these µ-receptors form, setting up the desire for the drug. Every hit sets up a positive feedback loop. You need it more and more.

Sully has done jail time twice for heroin. "Will you go back to it?"

"I realize that all my friends and some of my family members are into this stuff. I'd have to cut myself off from them completely. That's hard. How do you cut family out of your life?"

He seems resigned and then shares what he learned about how to make good choices from a drug boot camp he attended.

1. What is the best decision in the situation?
2. What are the consequences of the choice?
3. Can you stop and consider the ramifications?

This sounds like good strategizing. But what strategy is a person going to employ in the face of oncoming withdrawal? Replace heroin with water and imagine you're in a desert? Would you really care about these questions if all you could think about was intense thirst? The kind of thirst where your every thought is consumed by the idea of water? The reality is that drug addicts need to be in treatment programs in jail, programs that continue long after they are out. Without those programs, there will be more copper missing from empty buildings and more ruined lives.

The bigger context about drug addiction is that we are not going to solve anything by just managing the problem of addiction better. It is going to require a level of thinking that includes training people in new ways of being, rather than just targeting behavior. This means asking the kind of deep questions that get to the core of who people are, what they are committed to and what kind of a future they want to live into. Programs would have to be rooted in possibility and have clear measures for accountability. Punishment just reinforces all the ways of being that lead to becoming a repeat offender, chief among which is poverty. The "hard line punishment" people should check out the stats. They show that the private prison system is an abysmal failure, and the people in those facilities have not been helped.

The Affordable Care Act (ACA) was supposed to have included robust mental health programs, but that now seems a distant hope. Obama promised drug addiction treatment in the ACA, but it never materialized. In his first term Trump dismantled the funding for the ACA but offered no funding for heroin addiction. In 2016, heroin addiction had grown to become an epidemic that takes 64,000 lives per year.[8] The opioid epidemic decreased under Biden, but in 2025, as this book was going to press, Trump was dismantling the opioid monitoring centers and help centers offered through the CDC.

Weekend 7

Whistler must have been on vacation or something. I did not see him this entire weekend. But it was a relief to be greeted by an unfamiliar face. This CO was older, more relaxed, and seemed to have nothing to prove. He wasn't too worried about formalities. I was asked to strip, but I was allowed to keep on my underwear, socks and T-shirt. A small concession, but also a comfort to have something familiar in a place where everything is foreign and everything is tightly controlled. I was out of the holding pen quickly.

My compatriot did not fare so well. The laundry supplies were low. He did not get shoes and had to walk in stockinged feet to D-Dorm. As we trundled down the hall with our sleeping pads with sheets and blankets bundled inside, I heard him grumble under his breath: "These fuckers don't know what the hell they're doing." I kept my mouth shut and was thankful for the small gifts I'd received.

Every weekend the jail issues each inmate with a wristband that has a barcode on it, so your every movement is tracked when you're out of the cell. This week I was not issued one, but I did have the bracelet my daughter Rhéa made for me out of tiny rubber bands. A gift she got from Santa for Christmas. One would expect that this would have been considered contraband and promptly confiscated, but it seemed to be invisible to every CO I came across. I liked that. Rhéa, my little sweetheart so full of love, protected me every moment of my weekend.

I have absolutely no control over the TV selector. This process, from what I can tell, works according to the pecking order among big cats. It is clear to me that I'm at the bottom of the pecking order and I've got no seniority to make requests. I keep the peace and let the big cats hash it out.

On Saturday after lunch we were sitting on the bench watching a fight as usual, when Anton jumps up very animated and says, "You see that?"

"Huh? What?" I say. I'm completely clueless as to what he's talking about. It just looks like two guys bashing the crap out of each other.

"You're joking me? You didn't see that combination?"

"Combination?" I'm starting to get a little worried that I'm offending him with my stupidity about boxing.

Anton is a endomorph. That is a body type that is a little on the short side, but compact and strong. He stands about five foot six inches with a very muscular build. When I first entered D-Dorm, I thought, *My god, I hope I never get into a scrap with him.* It turns out that Anton is the sweetest, most generous guy in the whole dorm.

I try to catch up: "I'm sorry Anton, I don't follow boxing."

"Oh" Anton says, "while you were gettin' all smart and shit, I was coming up."

"You're a boxer?" I say.

Now he's got my attention. I'm very interested in his story. As I've gotten to know each of the guys in here, it is clear to me that none of them is beyond redemption, and my feeling is: "There but for the grace of God go I."

"Yeah, I trained in Catskill in the same gym where Mike Tyson trained."

"So, explain to me the combination."

"Well, when you're in the ring and the adrenalin is running high and you're getting your ass kicked, the coach will yell a combination of numbers from the sidelines. Like 1,1,4."

"That's code for what?"

"You see, each number is a punch. One is a jab. Two is a straight right. Three is a left hook and so on. When you've been knocked around in the ring, it makes it easy to remember what to do. When the coach yells 1,1,4 that means jab twice then right hook. He's telling me where the other guy's weak spot is. After training the punches over and over, it becomes second nature. It's like driving a standard transmission. You don't think about how to shift your car when you drive, it's 'automatic'." Anton smiles at his own joke. "You understand?"

I nod.

"So what did you see up there?" I point to the TV.

"Oh, he snuck one over the ref."

"How?"

"The short one is up against a guy with longer arms." Anton stands up and pretends he's the other fighter. He jabs me and keeps backing me up, while explaining: "He's going to keep taking shots to his head unless he gets in close. It's because he's built like me, all his power is up close in the body shots. He's got to stay away from a long punch or he's going see stars."

"... and what did the ref miss?"

"Oh yeah, the other guy is an orthodox fighter. The short one is a southpaw. When the southpaw pivoted and got in close, he hit him right in the abdomen, but then got him in the jaw with an upper cut and here's where he got sneaky. He elbowed him after the upper cut."

"Is that allowed?"

"Hell no! You see there's three kinds of guys that fight. Boxers, Fighters and Brawlers. That bit with the elbow, that's brawling. Muhammad Ali was a boxer. All jabs and lots of footwork, he'd never do that, but Mike Tyson would."

"What happened with you and boxing, Anton?"

"I just kept fucking up, but I'm done with that shit now."

"What's next for you?"

"I'm too old to be a boxer now, but I want to work with kids. Teach them how to work out and focus their minds on something. I was good, you know. I didn't get knocked out. I wasn't one of these brawler guys that would intentionally go in to get hit in the head just so they could hammer away at the other guy from the inside."

I look at Anton. He is a powerful man. The scars on his hands and his arms… I wonder where they came from. I am not going to ask. My gut sense is that he is proud and he'll tell his story when he feels the time is right. I know he's been through a shit storm, but he was clear that chapter was ending.

Ⅲ

Eben Alexander is a neurosurgeon who wrote *Proof of Heaven*, a first-hand account of his near-death experience after suffering from a rare bacterial brain infection from E. coli. A theme that runs through the book is: *You are loved and cherished, you have nothing to fear and there is nothing you can do wrong.* I sat and pondered this in the D-Dorm of the Columbia County Jail, wondering how the grand scheme of things related to my situation. I took stock of the men around me. What had I learned from them? What was I doing here? What effect were they having on my life? What could I do that would make a difference in their lives?

Like Anton, for example. He reflected my own prejudice back to me. I figured him for a thug when I first laid eyes on him. Discovering he wanted to help teach kids how to box was startling for me. Coming face to face with my own white stereotypical attitudes was disorienting. I realized Anton never had a chance to be seen.

One thing about being here that is coming through loud and clear is the humanity we share. In each of these men, I see the divine spark, what the Quakers call the Inner Light. It shows up in subtle ways like the gift of a sandwich or the way they gently showed me the ropes when I was a newbie. On the surface they seem gruff, but there is a softness in each of these men. We should foster that.

◫

I talk with Sully again. I ask him about his father.

"I have a strange relationship with my dad," he says.

"I sort of did too," I say, "until I realized that everything my dad did was his way of loving me. My dad was all about work. He made time for some things, but his work was his life. It engrained a work ethic in me even though I felt I did not have my dad as much as I wanted him."

He responds, "My dad left me when I was three. Things did not work out between him and my mother."

"You know, Sully, your life will never be complete until you get complete with your father." I just blurt it out. "I had to tell my own father some things that I'd been withholding for years before we got close."

"Oh, yeah? Like what?"

"Like how I felt he pushed me into chiropractic. Like how I never really had a choice about it. I know now that he only wanted the best for me and that for him chiropractic was a way for me to do good and have a good life. For years, I resented that I lived under this expectation."

"Mmmm." Sully nods.

"There are three things that can really fuck with relationships," I say to Sully. "Unfulfilled expectations, undelivered communication, and thwarted intention. If you really want to get at what is missing in life, at some point you're gonna need to look at these three areas with your dad. There is no going around it."

"I love my dad. I just don't know how to talk with him."

"It's not easy, but you just say what is right there. The

unvarnished truth. People yearn for that because it's real. And I'm not talking about dumping on someone. That's just mean."

Ⅲ

Listening in to me and Sully is a guy named Drew. When he was 18, he got into a fight on the streets in Hudson, NY over ten dollars. A friend he was with had been jumped and, like any good friend would do, Drew leaped into the fray to help. He grabbed his friend's assailant by the waist and carried him off like a sack of potatoes. What he didn't know was that the attacker had a knife. Drew was stabbed three times—once in the lung, once in the kidney, and once in the spine.

When I examined him, all three scars were clearly visible, but one thing I did notice was that the stab wound scar in the spine was just to the right of the Lumbar Mammillary Process. This saved him. The blade most likely hit the Process and then slid past the lamina pedicle junction and into the sacrospinalis muscle, missing the spinal cord and the lumbar nerve root. A few millimeters to the centerline and Drew would be in a wheelchair.

Drew described spasms on both sides of his lower back as well as burning pain down the L2 spinal nerve root after the accident. This made perfect sense, given where the entry wound was. The medical term for this is "referred pain." Nothing was wrong with Drew's leg, but the spinal dysfunction was activating the nerve at the level of the injury. He didn't take any medications to treat the pain and spasm now, because he'd gotten hooked on morphine at the time of the injury. After leaving the hospital, it was just a hop, skip and a jump from Oxycontin to heroin. It is not uncommon for addiction to start with prescription drugs and when the prescription runs out, the street is more than happy to provide what is needed.

Drew doesn't take any medication now, because he is afraid of addiction. Both morphine and heroin come from the opium plant. The difference is that morphine is a schedule 2 pharmaceutical and heroin is a schedule 1 illegal drug according to the DEA (Drug Enforcement Agency). Heroin is also about three times more addictive and can be combined (or cut) with many other drugs.

Giving people a bottle of highly addictive medication without other forms of therapy is, in my opinion, a massive mistake. If you only cover pain with medications, but look no deeper for causes, you end up with addiction. Drew did try Physical Therapy, but he got no results. Sadly, no one ever had the foresight to recommend chiropractic; that would have shown that Drew's pain was secondary to spinal joint dysfunction and the muscle spasm was not the source of the pain.

Once I put Drew through a rigorous range-of-motion exam, it became immediately apparent where the problems were. The area above and below the stab wound were locked up. It was as if Drew's body wanted that spot to continue to move by sacrificing movement elsewhere. The thing to do now was normalize movement up and down the spine. I did a chiropractic setup on lumbar vertebrae three and four and mobilized that area on both sides and then went to work on extension restrictions at thoracic vertebrae twelve.

"Man, that feels weird," Drew laughed, "but it feels good too."

"How often do you get the spasms and the burning down your leg?" I inquired.

"Twice a day. Sometimes more, but I just work through it. The way I figured, I'd just have to live with it for the rest of my life."

"Let me know how it feels on Sunday. If you get your 'normal' spasms."

"Okay, Doc. Thanks."

I didn't hear a peep on Sunday and noticed that Drew was doing sit-ups, something I'd never seen him try in his workouts over the last six weekends.

◫

The CO enters the cell and hears Fox News reporting on marijuana sales in Colorado. He says with glee, "Forty-three pot shops made a million dollars on their first day. No way the feds are going to shut that down. It is being taxed at 20 percent. That's good money for the government."

This starts up a lively discussion on the benefits of "medical marijuana." I know I'm going to be asked to weigh in on this topic, so I just hang back and listen to what comes up.

Most of the discussion revolves around cost. The cost of retail vs street cost. It turns out that the retail is only marginally more costly, and the consensus of the conversation is that it'd be better to pay the premium and avoid the legal hassles. I find this astonishing, given that all these guys are connected and know exactly how to land a dime bag if they want to, but they'd rather do it legal.

Strange to say, you can't buy legal marijuana in NY even though getting caught with small amounts is now only a health code violation, a ticket and a fine that amounts to something like a traffic ticket for parking on the pavement.[9] Seventy five dollars and pass jail without visiting.

Prohibition didn't work for alcohol and it certainly did not work for street drugs.[10] As a natural health practitioner, I'm in an unusual situation because I don't advocate for drug use of any kind, and that includes smoking, drinking, shooting or snorting drugs. But at the same time, I fully understand that the "war on drugs" is a "war on people with addiction problems."

Or, as the Steven Soderbergh's character Robert Wakefield clearly demonstrated in the film *Traffic:* "If there is a war on drugs, then many of our family members are the enemy. And I don't know how you wage war on your own family."

Americans are the source of the problem, not the drugs. We've locked up a lot of people and the lawyers and the prison corporations made a lot of money, but the government gets an "F" on providing a solution. What is it in our culture that we want to escape from with drugs? There is a fundamental problem deep at the root of American culture, a combination of spiritual vacuity and rampant materialism. It is played out in many more ways than drug abuse. *The Wolf of Wall Street* portrays money addiction. Pedophilia and sex addictions are another way to fill the void. Hoarding of stuff is yet another way to fill the vacuum of an empty spiritual life.[11]

It's 2:00 p.m. on Sunday. I'm feeling stir crazy. I can't find a comfortable place anywhere. I end up pacing the length of the dorm. This goes on for three hours.

When dinner finally arrives, we sit down. Anton looks me in the eye: "You okay, Doc?"

"Just a little stir crazy. I just want to get some fresh air. At this moment, I just can't stand to be all cooped up."

His face softens. I see his compassion. "I totally understand that."

Weekend 8

Juan and I, the two weekend prisoners, move through the big metal door separating us from the outside world, then through the metal detectors, and the sliding electric door. We are greeted by a CO we've never seen before.

He's all business and by the book. I'm asked to take a shower, something that absolutely disgusts me. You'd hate it too if you ever saw a shower stall in a jail. Imagine the bilge water that collects in the lower parts of a ship's hull and then add to that equal parts soap scum and fungi.

"I've never been asked to shower before."

"It's the rules. Everyone from the street takes a shower."

I try to argue my case: "I just took a shower two hours ago!" A hint of aggravation enters my voice and I immediately regret it.

"If you want to spend the weekend in the holding area then keep talking."

The part of me that hates rules and the irrational following of rules is about to burst out. The CO pushes the switch that turns on the shower and gives me a stern look: "Strip down and get in."

There is no negotiation going on here. He pulls the curtain and goes to the other side. I start to undress and weigh my options. I look up and see the camera. The eye of Big Brother is watching. I consider what I can do to comply with the rules and still keep myself from getting some nasty flesh-eating bug. I stand outside the shower cubicle, then, one at a time, I put my arms and legs in to get them wet. Then my head. I'm dripping wet.

The CO comes around the curtain to inspect my wet body for contraband and hands me a towel. The CO in the control room, the guy looking at the monitors, is either not watching or doesn't care. I've managed to keep out of contact with the floor of that shower cubicle.

"What size?" the CO says, referring to my clothes.

"Large."

"Shoes?"

"Ten."

The striped "pajamas" and the silly blue boating shoes arrive. I put them on and take my seat on the bench next to Juan. He shoots me a look that speaks volumes, which I interpret as: "Can you believe this fucking guy?"

Juan goes through the same routine. When he's done, we have to sit in the "electric chair"—a device which operates by magnetism. If we have any metal on our person, it lets out a loud alarm. Naturally, I feel as if I'm being violated, but the alternative of a body cavity search is even worse. Just as I think about what a cavity search would entail, I set the machine off and I can feel a bead of sweat form in my armpit.

"I think it's my cross," I say. I take off the cross and sit again. The alarm blares a second time. The CO pats me down and looks behind my ears and inside my mouth.

"Put your head here."

This machine also has a spot, a bullseye where you're supposed to stick your body part when the machine goes off. It's probably made by some military supplier. I put my chin on the bullseye and the machine goes off again.

"What's in your mouth?" the guard says, suspecting I'm hiding something.

"About seven thousand dollars worth of crown work," I say.

"Open your mouth again." He peers in like the dentist in *Marathon Man* and seems satisfied. In my head, I ask myself: "Is it safe?"

"What's your name?"

"Olejak O-L-E-J-A-K." I spell it because everyone seems to have the need to put a C in my name. He takes my locker key and the blue braided bracelet from Rhéa and puts them in what looks like a forensic evidence bag from *Crime Scene Investigators*. I'm sad to see the bracelet go, but I know Rhéa is with me in spirit.

"Grab your bunk and stand over by that door."

What continues to astound me is the variations in how things are carried out. This guy seems very interested in my mouth. Three weeks prior, a guard was interested in what I might be holding between the cheeks of my ass. Maybe the rationale is to just create uncertainty with the randomness of the intake protocol. The net effect is that no one seems to follow the official protocol keeping drugs and contraband out of the jail.

The CO finds a five dollar bill in Juan's shoe. What that's doing in there, I have no idea, because money has no value in this place. The currency is food. A bag of Doritos or Ramen Noodle Soup will get you a lot more mileage than a five dollar bill.

I've been asked by a number of inmates to bring in cigarettes and pot for them. My reply is always: "You're kidding, right? You know I'm a doctor who practices drugless healing. I'm the last person you'd want to ask."

◫

Standing outside the locked door to the innards of the jail, I can hear that stupid whistle of CO Whistler. Like a band with only one song in its catalog, Whistler keeps repeating this half-tune over and over. The door opens and there he is standing with his back to me on his little dais.

Whistler is six foot three inches, balding, with a pot belly: a "big man." The dais is a platform with a desk and the various switches that control the lights and the doors of A-Dorm and B-Dorm, the exits and entrance to the jail, and the medical office. I wonder if the needle on Whistler's broken record will jump to another groove if he bumps into the desk as he turns to unlock the door. No such luck.

Whistler is pulling a back-to-back two-day shift. I'm praying I get put back in D-Dorm, but it looks like I'm going to be quartered in B-Dorm with about sixteen other guys. My halcyon days in D-Dorm are over. I say halcyon because that is where the trusties live. As they are the guys that serve the food, that means more food on your tray at mealtimes and the possibility of a PB&J sandwich at night when your stomach starts to grumble. It also means you're not watched like a fish in a bowl.

B-Dorm, on the other hand, is a fish bowl. With glass on three sides, two cameras inside the dorm and the zone officer sitting at his throne, there is no place to hide. I have the bad luck of being placed in bunk #1, right next to the sink and the toilets. For 48 hours, my ears are assaulted with the constant flushing of toilets. The one advantage is that when the sinks and the showers are running, it does provide a pleasant kind of white noise that allows me to sleep.

Ⅲ

Saturday morning, 7:15 a.m. Breakfast arrives. Same deal. Rice Krispies, white toast, coffee, milk and juice. Carbohydrates all the way.

At 9 a.m., the commissary arrives. The other CO brings in large plastic bags of goodies that inmates have ordered. I finally got around to sending in a ten dollar money order to put some money on account. Anton, a trusty in D-Dorm, puts my order in on Wednesday for two legal pads and a pen.

Whistler enters the dorm to help pass out the commissary. Some guys have spent nearly two hundred dollars on extra food. He leaves the door ajar. A trusty walks the breakfast trays by the door and slams it shut. Whistler is now locked in a dorm with 18 guys and one other guard. He stops his inane whistling and yells through the plexiglass: "What'd you do that for, you little douche bag?"

The trustee just keeps walking with a smile on his face. He knows exactly how to push Whistler's buttons. I can see his face because of where I am, but Whistler can't.

Whistler yells again, "Hey, you know there's two of us in here." He's now locked in a dorm with 18 guys and one other guard. He's clearly not at ease. The other guard isn't worried and doesn't skip a beat. He has no worries. Without a zone officer on the block, Whistler has to go through the embarrassment of using his radio to have the central booking officer unlock the door. I've noticed that with officers who are respectful towards the inmates, this kind of mischief never happens. I've also noticed that Whistler's attitude actually puts himself and the other COs in an unsafe situation. It only takes a second for a fight to flare up, and he had to wait about three minutes for that door to unlock. This whole charade clearly demonstrates just how insecure Whistler is. All the bombast, the demeaning language, and the whistling too, are just attempts to put others off balance so he doesn't feel insecure.

Ⅲ

Edgar is a short little Black kid with a broken leg, wiry kinky hair and a big attitude. He talks in staccato Ebonics. I can barely make out every fifth word. He hobbles around the dorm like he's the mayor, and in some sense he is. He gets whatever he wants and it is clear he has leadership charisma. He's respected. I'm not sure why. I have a suspicion that his street reputation may have preceded him.

Whistler leaves once the door is unlocked and Edgar yells through the open door to a passing guard: "Hey, CO, tell one of them trusties I have something for him." It's not uncommon for food—the jail currency—to pass between cell blocks. There is horse-trading going on all the time.

Whistler, who is still within hearing distance, thinks the communique is for him and replies, "Tell him yourself," in a real smartass tone of voice.

Edgar retorts, "Shut up! Am I talkin' to you?"

Edgar sees right through Whistler's bombast and, broken leg or not, serves him up a full portion of mouth. The tone has the smoldering anger of the racial divide in this country. Whistler is a bigot, there is no doubt about that. He won't use the "N" word because he knows it will cause a riot, but in private, you know he's using all kinds of slurs as he talks about the Black people in the jail. I can see this in the dismissive way he treats these men, and in his body language as well.

Unsatisfied with the way he was treated, Whistler decides to have a go at me in the afternoon. I'm an easy mark sitting on my bunk, nose-deep in a book. I've got none of the swagger or toughness of these guys.

"Hey Olejak, make that bunk." My bunk has a sheet that is too short for the measly sleeping pad under it. One blanket is over my shoulders because it is cool in the dorm and the other is thrown carelessly on the end.

"I'm sitting on it."

"I don't give a rat's ass what you're doing on it. It's supposed to be made up when you're not sleeping. Read the sign on the wall."

"The sheet doesn't fit."

"Fix it up the best you can."

I straighten the blanket on the end and get back to my book.

"Hey, Olejak?"

I think, "Oh, please God, don't have him focus on me."

"Stevie Wonder could do a better job than that!"

I put the blanket over my legs and tuck the sides in under the pad. He seems marginally satisfied and leaves.

I get up and read the sign. In every dorm and every cell block, there is a square sign on the wall taped off with electric tape. There are laminated pictures showing how an inmate needs to dress, what a bunk should look like, how to hang your clothes neatly, how to keep your table.

The message under the picture of a neatly made bunk says: "Bunks should be made when not in use." The picture shows an empty bunk. I feel angry that I was singled out for harassment. I'm going to challenge him on it.

In B-Dorm there are three Black men and two Puerto Ricans. A strong in-group/out-group dynamic. When Edgar talks to Black and Puerto Rican men, he uses the term "nigger" nonchalantly as if it is not a racial slur. "Nigger" when used by a Black man to a Black man, is a form of solidarity. Even so, the repeated use of "nigger" bothers me.

Ⅲ

At 9:15 a.m., my package arrives. It's a book I ordered—*Quiet*, by Susan Cain. It explains what every introvert needs in order to function in a loud world.[12] I see myself all over the pages of this book. I am engrossed and enthralled by what I'm reading. It makes sense of why I feel so completely assaulted by the noise, the TV, the loud COs and the glaring fluorescent lighting.

The book made me see why when I host a party or give a public talk I often feel exhausted instead of energized. Why I shouldn't keep trying to act like an extrovert and rather take the time to appreciate my strengths as an introvert. I've learned to build down-time into my life so I can do public things and have something to contribute from a genuine inward place.

Cain's book makes me realize that I have to maintain my own integrity while I'm in here. I have to observe the humanity in all those around me, and not only in the inmates. I must engage as much as possible with the guards, even though they keep us at arm's length. I need to imagine how oppressed they must feel by having demands and requests made to them all day long. In ways I don't yet fully understand, I can see how stressful their jobs are. It turns out that COs suffer from all kinds of stress-related illnesses including cardiovascular disease, strokes and metabolic disorders.

◫

Austin and CJ had been getting on each other's nerves long before I got assigned to B-Dorm. I had no idea what was going on between the two of them. I did sense a kind of undertow in the room, but wasn't sure where the tension was coming from.

It started with yelling.

"You ain't my big brother! I'm my own man!" Austin yells, pointing at CJ.

The CO gets off his perch and came to the grille between the hallway and the dorm: "What's goin' on in there?"

Then Edgar steps between Austin and CJ and tries to de-escalate the situation. He says to them: "Hey man, cool it down or you're gonna have trouble. We don't want no trouble in here."

"It's cool," he says directly to the CO out in the hallway.

Next thing CJ takes a step toward Austin, like you'd see in a boxing ring, and taunts him.

"Fucking pussy!"

Austin steps back. "I don't like to fight."

"I like to fight."

Then like a bolt of lightning, CJ's fist hits Austin's ear, knocking him off balance.

I am just a couple of feet away when the punches start to fly. My first concern is for the safety of these guys. All it will take is one of them falling and hitting his head on the corner of a metal bunk, and it will be lights out.

For my own safety, I retreat to the corner of the dorm. In the flurry of testosterone and adrenaline, I think it better not to step between these guys or get caught up in what is coming.

"FIGHT!" The CO acting as zone officer sounds the alarm and six officers come running in at once and knock the two fighters to the ground.

"BREAK IT UP!" they yell several times. The struggle continues for a moment and then I hear, "I'm not resisting" from CJ, who is now face down on the cement with cuffs being put on him.

At the same time, I see Austin taking a blow from the sergeant we call Dinosaurus. The sarge blurts, "I'll fucking kill you." Austin is flipped over on his stomach and cuffs are put on him. Dinosaurus has a knee in Austin's back while two other COs hold him down.

All at once, the two fighters are grabbed by their shirts and roughly dragged to their feet. CJ's shirt rips in half. They are both pushed and shoved out of the dorm and as quickly as it started, the fight is over.

Like vultures going after carrion, some of the inmates grab CJ and Austin's stash of soups.

I ask Steve, the fellow next to my bunk, "What is going to happen to these guys?"

He tells me, "They'll probably get 30 days solitary."

The fight scared me, partially because it erupted so quickly and partially because I did not see it coming. I was frightened by the ferocity of the anger and what seemed to me like the excessive use of force to end the debacle. I did not feel safe after that.

A half an hour later, Austin is returned to the dorm. His head is down. He's bruised on his face and neck. He gets ostracized by the others because he didn't stand up to CJ. A little bravado might have ended in a stalemate. Saying you don't want to fight is a sure way to get in a fight.

No one is talking to him or looking at him. Edgar says: "Shit, man, what the fuck is wrong with you? I told you those motherfuckers were going to come in here and mess with you."

Austin doesn't say a word.

Once lunch is over, I go over to Austin's bunk where he has been eating his lunch by himself. I ask him: "Are you hurt?"

He's proud and says, "No, I'm fine." He does not want to admit any weakness in this crowd. And I don't blame him. I wouldn't either.

I press him a little and say, "Okay, well, if it hurts later, talk to me. I can help you."

I want to know more about how the fight started. "Why did you fight CJ?"

"I should have thrown the first punch," he says.

"Why?"

"He hit me, but he didn't have no power. If I would have thrown the first punch, he'd be down."

This makes sense. Like Anton, CJ is an endomorph. He's going to do much better with body shots and inside punches, whereas Austin is an ectomorph with longer arms. A single well-placed punch at the end of Austin's swing would be enough to have anyone seeing stars.

I think of what Mahatma Gandhi once said:"In a gentle way, you can shake the world."

I say: "Austin, do you know that I'm a Quaker?"

"No, what's that?"

"It's a faith that believes in many Christian ideas, but our main thing is that we feel very strongly about non-violence. We place a high value on peace and peaceful means of solving problems. That's why I'm in here, I refused to pay income tax because I was against the wars in Iraq and Afghanistan."

"Wow. For real? That's cool."

"Next time you want to throw the first punch, I want you to come and talk to me. Let's figure out a way to work it all out with words, okay?"

Austin nods.

Wally is a local farmer in Stuyvesant NY. He got drunk one night and beat up someone pretty bad. I ask him what he did before jail and he tells me about the heyday of his family farm where, he says, "We cleared one million a year."

I am surprised. "Are you saying a million net?"

He nods. "That was before everything went to shit."

"What happened?"

"In one year, we bought 300 cows infected with Salmonella and it went through the herd and wiped us out. Then we had a barn cave in under heavy snowfall and we lost another 159. Now all I've got is debt."

"So what are you doing now? Still dairy?"

"No, we raise beef cows now and have a little horseback riding stable. We call it TITS—Time In The Saddle. You like that? I made it up myself." He chortles.

Steve has lain motionless on his bed for most of Saturday and Sunday. Edgar hobbles over on his crutches to check on him.

"How's my man?"

"I'm alright."

"Come on, man. Don't bullshit me. You checked on me when my leg was all messed up and I was down." The one thing that Edgar has is people skills. He's a natural reader of people.

"I thought my kids would come and visit me today," Steve says. "It's my birthday."

"It's just another day, man. Don't let that shit get you down."

"Yeah, I know." The sadness is palpable in Steve's voice. There is so little to look forward to in this place. To see a familiar face and to know people on the outside are thinking about you is a big comfort.

Ⅲ

After dinner around 9:45 p.m., Austin comes over to where I am reading to strike up a conversation.

"What book you reading?"

"It's a book about introverts and extroverts."

"I don't know what that is."

"Edgar is an extrovert. Loud. Not shy. He has no problem getting right up in your grill. That kind of guy."

"Oh, yeah. I get that."

"And I'm an introvert. I sit and read all day. Kind of quiet. Think a lot. I was thinking about you and that fight today. You okay? Your ear was bleeding. You have quite a bruise on your neck."

Austin moves about, raising his arms above his head and moving his neck around as if to remove a kink. "Well I noticed my neck and back hurts. Sarge hit me in the head and shoved his knee in my back when I was on the floor."

"Yes, I saw that. I also heard Sarge say he'd kill you. Why?"

"I accidentally elbowed him when I went down. That's why he hit me. But he saw on the camera that I did not start the fight so he let it go."

"Let it go?"

"They couldn't charge me with assaulting an officer."

"Do you want me to help you with the neck and back pain?"

"Yeah. I saw you work on Edgar yesterday."

"I'm a chiropractor."

"Legit? You went to school and everything?"

"Yes, I've been working on people for over 25 years."

"It hurts when I turn my head from side to side." Austin points at a spot behind his neck just up from his shoulder blades. "And when I raise my arms and take a breath, it hurts too."

"So, let's work on it."

"You gonna crack me up like Edgar?"

"Yes."

"Well, you helped his sorry ass, so why not?"

"Sit down." I feel the muscles and joints of his back and what concerns me most right now is a fracture after trauma. I'm particularly concerned about broken ribs or a fractured spinus process, the part of the spine you can feel sticking out.

"Does it hurt here?" I push on the spinus.

"No."

"Here?" I rotate his torso to put pressure on his rib cage.

"No."

"How about here?" I feel a depression, the space between two adjacent vertebrae.

"No."

"How about off to the side?" I continue to poke around in the soft tissue to look for spasm and restrictions in the range of motion.

"It looks like T5 is out of position and not moving properly."

"What?"

"This bone right here," I poke, "is out of place."

A gallery of spectators is watching now. I feel like I'm in that Rembrandt painting with other medical professionals all looking on.[13]

"Hey, guys. Stand over there." I motion to the window. They immediately understand and block the view.

"Austin, you ready?"

Before he can answer, it's over. Without a beat, I perform what is known as a short-lever high-velocity thrust to Austin's back to set the joint that is out of position and moving errantly.

Austin cries out in shock and surprise, not knowing what just happened. He looks a little spooked.

"Stand up. Move around."

He stands and stretches and discovers he can take a breath for the first time since the fight without a pain between his shoulders.

"You good?" I ask him.

"Yeah, Doc. All good."

"Lie on your back. Let's sort your neck out too."

There is a moment when I am examining Austin's neck when he looks me right in the eye. For the first time, I really see him. See him like the Navi see each other in the film *Pandora*. There is trust there. This, to me, is the greatest gift—to receive the trust of another person. It is as if Austin is saying to me, *I'm letting my guard down for you. I'm trusting that you are going to take care of me, don't disappoint me.*

"Turn your head left."

"Now right."

"Does that hurt when I bend it that way?" I'm holding Austin's neck bent to one side at about 45 degrees, right at the end of what would be considered a normal passive range of motion.

"Yeah, right there. That is painful." And that is precisely where the bruise is.

"All right, let's finish this."

In quick succession, I release the right and the left side.

Austin cries out again, followed by hooting and howling from the peanut gallery.

"Shhh," I admonish them.

Austin is lying still on his back. "Take a few deep breaths," I instruct him. "How's that feel now?"

"I feel so relaxed."

I slide my left hand under his back and place my right over his heart. "Keep taking deep breaths. Close your eyes. You feel any emotions coming up?"

"No."

"Any anger or upset regarding the fight?"

"No." I can't quite tell if he's in touch with the emotion or not so I let it go, worried that a guard might come in and destroy the moment of healing.

"You can just rest for a bit. If you want to sleep, that'd be very healing too."

Another inmate asks Austin, "You okay, dude?" Probably because he's been very still since I worked on his neck.

He opens his eyes momentarily and smiles, "I can breathe."

When Austin wakes up, I check in with him again. "How's it going?"

"Great. I want to show you something." He reaches into the little metal desk bolted to the floor and pulls out a plastic bag with two pictures in it: "That's my wife." And turning to the next photo: "That's my son."

"You have a beautiful family. Thank you for sharing that."

"I should have my wife see you. Where is your office?"

"In Delmar."

"Is that far from here?"

"Not too far—about half an hour."

"She broke her pelvis in a car crash a year and a half ago. She was out with my brother-in-law and it was icy in Brooklyn. He lost control of the car and another car crashed into them. She was in the hospital for a long time, then had a body cast. Now she's in pain all the time."

He looks lovingly at the picture again and speaks softer now, sadness creeping into his voice.

"After she left the hospital and was healed, we tried to have another baby. She was five months pregnant when she miscarried."

He puts his arms to his chest as if he is cradling a baby. "It happened at home. The baby was alive. I held it to my chest, but it was blue. I could feel her heart beating, but then after a minute it was weak and then stopped. I felt her last heartbeat and then she was gone."

Tears are streaming down my face at this moment. The TV is loud and the guys are engrossed in the football game.

"My wife should see you. I know she lost that baby because of the accident. The damage to her pelvis."

All I can say is: "It's possible."

In B-Dorm, there is an unspoken pact among inmates: "When I'm doing my 'business,' you back off and leave me in peace." Everyone observes it. If you need to pee while someone is having a "sit down," you wait.

Keenan is a big Black man, an endomorph with a big chest, big arms, and big shoulders. In a word, solid. And he is also a man who expects a modicum of dignity in a place that offers very little of that.

The toilet in B-Dorm is called The Head—like on a boat—and it consists of two toilets marked "P" and "S". If you need to do #2, you use the head marked "S" and you don't mix it up. As Keenan told me when I arrived, "That's just how we do it in here."

Whistler entered the dorm at the beginning of his second shift and right off the bat starting in on Keenan when he was taking care of his "business."

"Take that blanket down."

"Come on, a man needs a little privacy!"

"Not my problem, you could hang yourself in there."

"Really? Where am I gonna hang myself? The only thing in here is the toilet!"

"I don't want no liability."

Keenan finishes up, but does not remove the blanket. Whistler waits, annoyed. "Come on. What are you doin' in there?" as if to insinuate Keenan is doing some bizarre act other than dealing with a bodily necessity. Whistler leaves and the dorm breathes a collective sigh of relief.

The guys begin immediately to grouse among themselves about what just happened. The consensus is that Whistler must be a homosexual because he is so interested in what is going on behind the improvised stall door. They all laugh together and Max chimes in: "Whistler is an asshole, but at least he's not as big an asshole as Miles."

Another guy interjects: "Yeah, they're both assholes, but Miles is the worse of the two evils."

Ⅲ

WEEKEND 9

Joseph Olejak
323 Delaware Ave.
Delmar NY 12054

Jan 21, 2014

Columbia County Jail
D Dorm
85 Industrial Tract
Hudson NY 12534

Dear Bobby,

I just wanted to let you know how much I appreciated the conversation we had in D-Dorm when the block was empty on Saturday.

When we connected, it was clear to me you really love the woman in your life, you are committed to a rewarding career, and you are a generous person.

I acknowledge that you are faced with some challenges to fulfilling those desires. At this moment there is a sort of internal fight going on between a self (we could call this your lower "s" self) that has pulled you in the direction of drugs, and all the trouble that entails, and the Self (we could call this your higher, capital "S" Self) that has you striving for something better.

I want you to know that from this point forward, I'm only going to relate to the Bobby that is Love, Generosity, and Freedom.

This is the person that shone through to me. In the Quaker faith, we'd call this higher Self shining through an expression of The Inner Light. We all have this inner beauty and the more we allow its expression, the more it grows on us.

I also want you to know that I'm here to support you in any way I can to assist you in achieving what is most important to you and your life. That could be listening, it could be sharing my own experience, or it could be pointing you in the direction of resources and people.

One thing we talked about was the Landmark Forum, a powerful three-day course that has you get really connected with what YOU want. In February and through May, Landmark will be offering an introduction to the Landmark Forum in Albany and I'd be honored if you'd be my guest at that event. You could see for yourself what is possible out of participation in the program.

Another invite I'd like to extend is to the Quaker Meeting in Old Chatham, Sundays at 11 a.m. I won't be there until after May 18th but as a person who shared a cell with me, you'd be most welcome. The service is quiet and an opportunity to listen to that inner voice that is love, generosity, and freedom.

Warm regards,
Joseph

Weekend 10

On Wednesday, I mailed myself *Long Walk to Freedom* by Nelson Mandela. The timing of mailing is crucial because the person who does the mail sorting here doesn't care. If a book arrives and you are not actually in the jail at the time, you can find your book gets tossed, lost, or stolen. There does not seem to be a very high level of accountability for prisoner property unless the inmate is insisting on it.

The book arrived on Saturday and at 9 a.m. it landed in D-Dorm. I was pleased, because the stash of books in my locker was getting low. I had been able to snag *Adirondack Stories*, and also *The Guernsey Literary and Potato Peel Pie Society* by Mary Ann Shaffer and Annie Barrows. Inmates are not supposed go to someone else's locker and choose books they want. Some guards try to make sure an inmate can have some say in the selection of things out of their locker, but others can be downright nasty about it.

This weekend my intake CO was Nola. He's okay about such things. I was thankful for that. As a general rule I try not to ask for anything I don't really need. Other inmates, like Billy, seem to ask for lots of stuff, figuring that will get you at least some of what you ask for. This seems to depend largely on the CO. Some are just more generous than others. I've figured out which COs are generous and I limit my requests to them.

This weekend was a bit hard on me emotionally. Even though it was weekend 10, which heralded the one-third mark through my sentence, I felt rather empty, lethargic, and hopeless. In spite of this, the weekend flew by, and it seemed that no sooner had I arrived than it was Sunday night.

Some of those feelings might have just been purely physiological. I had a slight fever when I arrived on Friday and

I was fatigued. On Saturday and Sunday, the fever had not progressed to flu-like symptoms, but remained a low-grade feeling of the blahs. I slept longer than usual. And while I needed the rest, sleeping on the steel rack generated complications with my back—numbness and tingling down my left leg.

One great thing about the weekend was the care I received from the men in the dorm. Several of them—Anton, Drew, and Robert—asked me if I was okay or if I needed anything. They could sense I was a bit "off my feed" as it were. It was very sweet. At one point, Anton made tuna salad and crackers from a concoction of ingredients in his commissary and offered me two crackers.

Because of how I was feeling, I was not really able to connect emotionally with any of the men in the dorm, but I was okay with that. It seemed like a natural organic rhythm, a natural ebb and flow from the intense connection that I had had in the past few weekends.

I managed to read about two hundred pages of Mandela's autobiography, *Long Walk to Freedom.* Such a book puts one's life in perspective. I knew about some of the repressive measures the apartheid government had inflicted on Africans, Indians, and Coloureds (people of mixed race) in South Africa, but I had no idea of the lengths to which the Afrikaners went to dominate and control the native people and ethnic minorities like Indians and Chinese. I worry about this kind of repression returning to America.[14]

What I found so courageous about Mandela was his willingness to sacrifice his own life for something bigger than himself. I worry that we are running out of people like him. In the United States, we have become too materialistic and apathetic to care, even about matters that concern our own self-interest. If the highest goal we can attain is personal comfort, then the promise of our Constitution is lost. I read that Mandela worked a job for £2 a month—about $53 in today's money—and went to night school to attain his law degree, studying by candlelight because a kerosene lamp was too expensive, and then hoofed it for three miles to get to work every morning. I was astonished by his inner drive and willingness to take on greater and greater risks.

After attaining success as a lawyer and making a difference for fellow Africans, he became a member of the inner circle of the outlawed African National Congress. He did it because, in his words, "When a man is denied the right to live the life he believes in, he has no choice but to become an outlaw." He was later banned from participating in any form of gathering, and then given a lifelong prison sentence. None of this stopped him from advocating for something bigger than himself. All of that in lieu of a quiet life and a comfortable law practice.

Who in the United States is willing to take such risks today? Daniel Ellsberg, Julian Assange, Chelsea Manning, and Edward Snowden are a few notable whistleblowers who have had the courage to expose corruption.[15]

Many of the questions these whistleblowers raised are also central to my Quaker Witness. As the IRS tax deadline of April 15th approaches again, I have to face the question of what I am willing to pay for. How do I reconcile my conscience with the unacceptable deal I'm being asked to make? Words and actions have to align if there is to be integrity in the world. What could be a simpler expression of truth than the alignment of words and action? I support my tax money going to social security for pensioners, but I don't support the continued occupation of countries the US has invaded. I support roads and bridges that don't fall down, but don't support the F35 Fighter Jet.

I support food stamps, but find drone strikes horrific.

What does better look like? For me, it would include federal legislation that allows persons of conscience to pay a Peace Tax—a separate income tax that supports all the needs of the country except war.[16] We need to examine the worn-out notion that war is a solution to problems. The liabilities and legacy of war should be clear at this point in history—they form a cycle of perpetual suffering and violence.

With each breech of integrity around our values, it becomes easier and easier to slide into atrocity—drop an atomic bomb, commit an act of mass murder, invade a country that does not possess weapons of mass destruction—and it becomes easier for the world to view such events as acceptable within the realm of warfare. But as Mandela writes, "Everyone says something is impossible, until it becomes possible."

In many countries, it has been universally acknowledged for centuries that conscientious objection to war is an acceptable form of protest. It is enshrined in the laws of countries worldwide, including our own. Why shouldn't we demand that our money must not be conscripted for war, as an acceptable form of conscientious objection?

Weekend 11

This weekend was the most boring of all the weekends here so far. As a result, my mind began to turn over all the loose ends in my life that have been unraveling since I began my jail sentence. The frayed edges are many and are getting more and more difficult to manage as time marches on.

It feels like I'm inside the Joseph Heller novel, *Catch-22*. In the novel, Yossarian, a bomber pilot, is required to fly dangerous missions where the possibility of being killed is high. He knows when he reaches a certain number of sorties, he'll be allowed to go home, but every time he gets close to finishing his tour of duty, his commanding officer raises the number of missions. The central question in Heller's book is "What does a sane man do in an insane society?"

My life experience is not that dissimilar from Yossarian's. I could pay the tax and keep on being a good and compliant US citizen, but then I'd be faced with the ongoing dilemma of my complicity in supporting war. Getting out of the system's rules is like the Catch-22 clause in Heller's novel; as soon as you start to remove yourself, life gets crazy. The people inside the system think you're nuts, while you experience yourself as finally getting sane. You are compelled to get out because you just can't support how vast sums of money are being spent.

My situation was becoming more insane by the day. I took a decision which for me was a sane response to violence, but the price has been very high. The sums I have been required to pay—restitution to the court, keeping current with taxes, paying child support, paying lawyers to manage this giant mess, maintaining an apartment, and staying current with business expenses—are completely unmanageable. And added to that the Federal Court, by refusing to allow me to work on certain weekends, has caused a severe drop in my income. I now have far more debts than there will ever be money to pay them.

On Saturday night, I could not fall asleep. My mind kept turning over all these things. How am I going to manage all this?

On top of all this, I have begun to worry about my own health. In the past four weeks, my chest has been so tight at times I've wondered: Am I having angina? A heart attack? It is a comfort to know some physiology, and I have had to continually remind myself that it is just fear. But fear is real emotion and it can make the things one fears appear very real.

When I feel scared or fearful, I have to remind myself to stick to the present moment. Deal with what is at hand. Take care of the present and the tomorrows will take care of themselves.

It's Superbowl Sunday. The way I feel is: Who cares?

Nevertheless, there is a great deal of fanfare here in D-Dorm about who will win the big game. Will Peyton Manning end his career with a Superbowl win or will the Seattle Seahawks rout the Broncos?

It's all "bread and circuses," a distraction for the masses. The Superbowl doesn't want people to think about anything that would actually change the quality of their life. It's just a great opportunity for advertisers to add more wants and desires to the psyches of people so they can pedal the economic treadmill they are on, and obtain more stuff they don't really want or need.

One hopeful sign was the dude who barged into the post-game interview and grabbed the microphone to say: "Investigate 9/11! It was perpetrated by our own government!" At least that was some balance to the constant Navy ads spouting how they are "a force for good" with stern-faced young men and women saying how they will "obey those above who command them." Talk about state-sponsored propaganda! Why waste time with double-think when we can skip right to direct indoctrination?

Weekend 12

Up at 7 a.m. and eat. Sweep the dorm. Take out the breakfast trays. Mop the floor. Three-hour break. Lunch at noon. Take out trays. Write a letter. Read a book. Play chess. Have a conversation. Watch the TV. Wait for dinner. Eat dinner, exercise. Lights out at 11 p.m.

Because this rhythm is divorced from any useful activity, one barely notices time. In fact, it is better for the mind to ignore the passage of time. The only way to mark time, if you wanted to, is to observe the comings and goings of the guards as they come in to do their counts every 30 minutes on the quarter and three-quarter hour.

Occasionally, when the clouds have lifted, I see the sun setting through the barred windows. When one has nothing to do but kill time, it is possible to watch the arc of a setting sun one degree at a time, and notice each subtle change in the hue of the sky as the sun's rays move across a masonry block wall.

The weekends are going smoother and faster now. Inmates and COs know me. I've become a known quantity, respectful of the rules and no trouble. As such I'm left alone, which is the way I like it.

▥

Sochi Winter Olympics: I have respect for the intensity and commitment of Olympic athletes. To single-mindedly train to be at the top of the top in an area of competition is really inspiring. Most of these Olympians are young people under the age of 20. For the few who doggedly beat back the hand of time and dare to compete at the age of 35 (the Russian figure skater) or 43 (the Czech biathlete)—those people have guts. They literally "gut it out" to get to the finish line with almost nothing left but pure adrenaline and a will to win. Powerful stuff.

Skiers are tested on the slopes. Will they put the last measure of themselves into the sport for the gold? Will they hold back? And behind the scenes, what is the commitment? Who is supporting these athletes?

For myself, identifying with Quaker principles feels very similar. It is a solo act, but yet the community watches, weighs in like a coach, and from the stands asks important questions of the person who is on the court. It reminds me of these lines from Rumi's poem *The Fragile Vial:*

> A True Man stares at his old shoes
> and sheepskin jacket. Every day he goes up
> to his attic to look at his work-shoes and worn-out coat.
> This is his wisdom, to remember the original clay
> and not get drunk with ego and arrogance.
>
> To visit those shoes and jacket
> is praise.
>
> The Absolute works with nothing.
> The workshop, the materials
> are what does not exist.
>
> Try and be a sheet of paper with nothing on it.
> Be a spot of land where nothing is growing,
> where something might be planted,
> a seed, possibly, from the Absolute.[17]

I am particularly drawn to this line: "The Absolute works with nothing."

When I think of being an inmate in a jail, the word "fallout" comes to mind. Not nuclear fallout but an emotional black rain. It is what happens to others in the absence of the jailed person. It can be sadness, loneliness or just plain fear. It affects adults and children alike, although children, I think, feel it differently. For them it's more like a nagging worry.

It's not just the ones left behind at home that feel it. The inmate concerned feels it too. It emerges at unexpected moments in the form of rancorous emotions leaking out at inopportune times. It can descend like a black cloud or suck all the air out of your lungs. It's the panic you feel when it all becomes just too much and you feel like nothing is going to work out.

There are no remedies for this type of fallout. You don't want to share it too much because if it gets on others they can get scared and angry too. The best way to deal with is to get quiet and alone and listen for direction. It just breaks down slowly on its own over time.

Weekend 13

It's been my thirteenth weekend—the halfway point. The inertia of getting through all this seems to be lifting. The warp of time is now shorter. The days are longer. The snow falls outside D-Dorm and icicles hang low off the roofs.

The weather is warming, and so by evening, the slow drips are sharpening the icicle ends. Drip. Drip. Drip. Like the seconds ticking off a clock as the second hand clicks inexorably towards six o'clock.

At 5:45 p.m., I ready myself for leaving. The same routine since the first weekend: brush my teeth, straighten my hair (as best I can without a comb), fold my sheets, towels and blankets, roll the whole business up in the absurd sleeping pad with my cup and spork (a ridiculous bendy plastic spoon-fork combo), and wait. If the guard is sitting in his seat, I send him mind-messages while he stares at the internet.

Today my mind-messages say: "Look at the clock! Let Olejak out! Unlock the door!"

The phone rings. The guard picks it up and writes something in his log book (Release Olejak, and the time—I'm guessing). He walks over to the door and lets me out. My telepathic powers are working!

The CO unlocks the door and says: "See you next weekend. How many more you got?" I smile. "Thirteen. I'm out on May 18th."

I make my own "long walk to freedom" down two corridors to Central Booking and the holding pen. I see faces behind plexiglass windows looking at me. Some are strangers. Some I've come to know. Some I've even helped.

Shoe gives me the peace sign with a great big smile. He clearly gets me.

One yells: "Take it easy, Doc." I shoot a high five.

Another shouts to the CO: "Let me out with Doc, I'll come back!"

The guard laughs. "You got stuff you want to keep in your locker?" he says to me.

"Yes, thank you—these books here." I put *The Path to Love* by Deepak Chopra and *Empire of Illusion* by Chris Hedges on the zone officer's shelf. We have an easy back and forth now. A little bubble of trust is growing between us, which I appreciate.

It feels so much more human than the day I first walked in, when all I felt was fear and uncertainty.

A story

A tourist walking along a remote stretch of Mexican coast comes upon a sea surge that has washed thousands of starfish onto the sand. They are drying out in the sun and will surely die.

The tourist picks one up and tosses it back in the ocean. A fisherman sees this and as the tourist approaches, he says in broken English: "You're wasting your time. There are thousands of them. You'll never be able to save them all."

The tourist bends down, picks up another starfish, and throws it back into the Pacific. "I made a difference to that one!"

My starfish is a kid called Drew. There are 140 inmates in the Columbia County Jail. I've interacted with maybe 30 since I've been here, but if I've made one real connection, it's with Drew.

This past Sunday was the last day of his four-month stint. Over the 13 weeks, I've learned a lot about his life. He shared his story because I listened without judgment or advice. Drew is a good kid and with the right coaching, he is going to make good on his promise: "I'm done fucking up."

Drew got six months for blowing his paycheck on drugs instead of giving money to his kids. It's not an uncommon situation in here. The bad news is that once you get behind in child support and get put away for six months, it becomes a downward financial spiral that is nearly impossible to recover from.

This Thursday, the Landmark Integrity Course starts in Albany. It is a ten-session program exploring what integrity means. Not as a character trait, but from the standpoint of "what's missing for workability in life." Workability for a bicycle is two wheels, a seat, a chain, handle bars and pedals. Integrity is to life what these things are to a bike.

Drew is now out of jail and I've invited him to the Introduction to the Landmark Forum. We have already talked about the course at length and he's even filled out his application form. What he hopes to get out of it is a kind of sacred compact that he's making with himself. He must reveal to the world the future he wants to live into. This declaration must be his task because, by his word, it will empower him to alter reality.

The challenge that I see with so many of the people in this jail is that they see themselves as "damaged." They are living inside a story that "damaged goods are good for nothing." Broken. They have passed judgment on a single act or series of acts. They describe themselves as "scumbags," "fuck ups," or "losers." For them the first step on the path to integrity—life workability—is to begin describing their lives in terms of what is possible rather than a future that is just an extension of the past. As Chopra says: "We (human beings) are a field of pleuripotentiality where anything is possible." This is my hope for Drew.

Ⅲ

Another inmate who I hope will not be broken is Pitt. Pitt got kicked off the "trusty ward" aka D-Dorm, the place where you go if you are one of the inmates who serves food or does other chores in the jail. In D-Dorm, you get to have more freedom of movement and some extra time in the recreation yard.

Pitt ratted out a guard who was sleeping while on duty. It was stupid really, as it was none of his business. He said something to another guard, it got back to a supervisor, and the guard got reprimanded. After that, the axe fell on Pitt.

As punishment, they have put Pitt in I-block, the isolation area. He would have a cell to himself for 30 days. Maybe some pensive time will humble him a bit. I felt sad for him as he packed up his stuff and carried it down the hall. His cheeks were flushed red as he did the walk of shame. Some of the guys said encouraging things as he left: "You'll be back— don't sweat it." And "Hang in there, 30 days goes fast."

Things do go fast. Jail can be put to productive use if you have books and the discipline to study. I am thankful to all the friends and Friends (Quakers) who have sent books.

WEEKEND 14

When I arrived in the jail this weekend, I was surprised to find some new faces in the little cloister of D-dorm. Len and Jacob were the new residents. Even Pitt, who earlier had managed to get himself evicted from D-dorm, had found a way to get back in the good graces of the CO who had downgraded him to solitary. We were a full house.

A (short for Ari) had been my bunk mate—lower level—for the last five weekends. However, this time he was not happy to see me. I liked to sleep in the top bunk above A because that bunk is the only one in the dorm that is not directly under a bank of buzzing fluorescent bulbs. When I entered the dorm, he said: "You're over there this weekend because of that cookie under my bed."

I had foolishly dropped a cookie from my bunk last weekend and it fell along the wall and landed on the floor under the bunk. A was unhappy because he felt it would attract spiders. A is Black, I'm white. I have always felt he has a bit of a chip on his shoulder toward me, and I've never been sure if he just dislikes me or if there is a bit of racism there.

"I'm sorry about that, T. I realized I lost the cookie, but I couldn't find it. I don't want there to be any bad feelings between us. What can I do to make it up to you?"

T softened a smidge. "It's okay."

"Are you sure? We're good? I promise that won't happen again."

"We're good."

Troy, Coleman, and Anton call themselves the Three Gorillas of D-Dorm. They are all big, strong, Black men. Men you definitely don't want an argument with. Troy was a fighter. Coleman has biceps the size of my thighs, and A reminds me of a bomb about to explode. There seems to be a very sweet side to Anton when I hear him talking about his wife and kids, but I also have the feeling he could explode if provoked.

I'm happy the cookie situation was defused.

My first patient for the weekend was Finn. A kid in jail for DWI—Driving While Intoxicated. He's a landscaper and a tall guy, thin and wiry. He's been in jail for about a month awaiting transfer to a DWI bootcamp program. His upper back curves forward as if he's lifted one too many pieces of sod. He's an easy chiropractic case. At 25 his spine is still very pliable, and within minutes I'm able to restore the motion to the restricted parts of his spine.

The next one was Jacob. I first met Jacob on December 20th, on my third weekend on G-block. He was brought into the jail with 18 others who had been swept up in a drug cleanup operation conducted by the Hudson Police. I only saw him twice that first weekend. He was in bad shape, and going through the hideous effects of heroin withdrawal. His cell was two doors down from mine, and what I heard was mostly moans and coughing. When I did get out of the cell for meals, I noticed he was lying under blankets in the fetal position. At the time, I did not completely understand what he was experiencing. After talking with Sully in D-dorm at length about the effects of heroin on the human body, I now understand clearly the pain and suffering Jacob experienced that weekend.

When I was in G-Dorm, I had initially refused to treat Jacob because I did not have the legalities covered with the informed consent form. A lawyer would say I was being smart, but in retrospect, given the condition Jacob was in at the time, it does not feel good that I withheld help when I could have done something to ease his pain.

Jacob told me that when he heard he was being picked up by the police, he prepared himself for withdrawal as best he could by swallowing a balloon filled with Suboxone (Buprenorphine) tablets. It is a semi-synthetic opioid that is used to treat opioid addiction in dosages higher than 2 mg.

I asked him why he'd gone to such lengths to deal with the problem of withdrawal. He explained: "The jail does not offer any treatment for heroin addiction for at least three days after you arrive. The worst part of withdrawal happens in the first three days. If you've never experienced withdrawal, you just can't imagine how bad it is... you just want to die."

I looked into how bad heroin withdrawal can get, and I was shocked. The worst physical symptoms include akathisia (uncomfortable feeling of inner restlessness), bone pain, chills (shivering), cramps, diarrhea, difficulty sleeping (insomnia), dizziness, flu-like symptoms, general feeling of being unwell (malaise), headaches, joint pain, muscle pain, nausea, sweating, tachycardia (rapid heartbeat), and vomiting. The psychological symptoms include anxiety, cravings for the drug, concentration problems, confusion, depression, feeling agitated, feeling irritable, panic attacks, paranoia, and thoughts of suicide.

"So you just wait for the balloon to come out the other end?"

"Yup. It's not pretty, but you do what you have to—to survive."

Jacob had been able to soften the blow of withdrawal through what he'd "hooped." Hooping is the technique of shoving what you need in your ass to get it into the jail. Jacob said that, after withdrawal, he felt like he was not getting enough oxygen to his brain. He described it as "foggy and fuzzy." I'd read about this in the literature, but never come across it in practice. After I administered the chiropractic adjustment, he felt what he described as "clarity" and could "think clearer."

I explained to him that this was a stress response from the nerves in his neck that control blood supply to the head and neck. Stress, subluxation (misalignment resulting in altered nerve tone), or even anxiety could trigger a stress response that could cause a lack of blood flow to his brain.

Jacob is 47 years old. No family still alive. No friends that I could figure. He is alone in the world. But what was compelling about this man was his need to connect with other people on a heart-to-heart level.

In retrospect, I was amazed by the power of what we Quakers call a declaration. I had declared many times in Meeting (quietly connecting to Spirit) and to others in conversations that I would experience a transformation when I was in jail. I was not disappointed.

Jacob and I talked for hours by the dorm door leading out to the recreation yard. It was winter and the door was closed due to drifting snow and ice. Fortunately this door allowed a tiny draught to leak in from a broken part of the insulation in the door jamb. It was the only place in the dorm where one could breathe fresh air. One Saturday, I was happily surprised by the smell of warmish air and melting snow leaking through the door as the temperature outside rose to 50 degrees. I watched little rivulets of water trickle down from the roof, hit the pavement, and work their way under a patch of ice in oblong goblets drifting off to parts unseen.

Jacob's story was one of substance misuse, the new and less pejorative term now listed in DSM-V[18] for what used to be called substance abuse. It was a long story that stretches back to the 1980s and military service. Jacob calls himself an addict, and when he talks about drugs, he gets excited and animated as he regales me with stories about the effects of drugs on his life. He often pauses and reels himself back in saying: "See, right there, I was glorifying it again. That's bad shit. I shouldn't do that. That's the addict talking."

Jacob had been charged with five counts of dealing drugs. At one point he hands me the indictment and asks me to read it.

"None of that shit is true." He points right at me, emphatic. "Don't get me wrong. I bought drugs but I never dealt drugs. I was caught up in this sting operation."

"It says here you sold heroin to an undercover police officer and they have it on video. That's seems pretty black and white."

"Yes I did that, but there is other stuff that is not on the video."

"Like what?"

"Like Del (the drug dealer that Jacob got his dope from) telling me he would not sell me my fix unless I passed his dope to the person in the car. I didn't know who she was. I was used."

"The indictment says you profited from the sale. Is that true?"

"It's true that I took the money, but I had to give it back to Del or he'd cut me off. He betrayed me. He must have known what was going on and he set me up."

Jacob's voice goes up a bit. He's angry.

"Well, that may be so, but what is also true is that you were operating in a world of drugs where that kind of thing is routine, no?"

Jacob looks at the floor. "You remind me of something the pastor told me during church services in this jail. If you hang out in a barber shop long enough, eventually you're going to get a haircut."

I laugh. "I like that. I'd put it this way. You are *cause* in the matter of your own life. And the most powerful thing you can do is acknowledge the role you played in being a part of it. Not right or wrong, but factual."

He puts the indictment away and I notice a Bible in his

drawer along with a book called *Living Sober.*

I say, "I want to show you something. What I think is the most powerful passage in the Bible."

"Revelation?"

"Revelation is about apocalyptic destruction and the coming of a new world order. I was thinking about the Gospel of John where it says: *In the beginning was the Word, and the Word was with God, and the Word was God.* On one level, this passage is about creation of the world, but it is also about creating with your own word. If you believe that God dwells in each of us and that by Word, God created all that there is, it also makes sense that we can be creators with our word too."

There is a long pause in our conversation.

"Jacob, words tumble out of our mouths, but we don't treat them with respect. We relate to them like 'talk is cheap'. What if we related to our word like it had the power to create whole new worlds?"

He says, "I really appreciate what you're saying. I was beginning to lose hope. You know when a person loses hope, they just want a way out."

"I'm glad I was able to listen and respond with something useful. Regardless of what happens, you can always count on me to support you however I can."

As I said this, I recalled Psalm 119: 'Thy word is a lamp unto my feet, and a light unto my path.'

The whole time I was talking with Jacob I was looking at the inside of his right arm. A very big scar there.

"I had an accident there," he says vaguely.

"Work related?" The scar is a big triangle on the inside of his arm.

(It looked to me like compartment syndrome, by the size of the scar. This is a condition in which there is increased pressure in a limb where blood supply is cut off. Quite often the limb needs to be cut open to relieve the pressure, resulting in a very large scar.)

He is suddenly ashamed. "Okay, I'll tell you about it. The first few times I shot heroin, I wasn't very good at using a needle. I poked through the vein and my arm got infected. After a few days, it turned septic and I almost lost my arm."

"You're a lucky guy!"

"You're not kidding. The doctor said if I'd have waited a day longer, I might have even died from blood poisoning."

"What was it like, having your arm get infected from a bad needle jab?"

"It was the most disgusting thing I've ever had to deal with. I was on the verge of going through withdrawal and my arm was twice its normal size filling up with pus."

"What happened?"

"The doctor, in his office, drained some of the fluid off with a syringe and then he admitted me into the hospital. I spent four days there with a tube in my arm."

"How was that?"

"It was the most painful thing I've ever experienced. Every day they inserted this tube and squeezed my arm to reduce the swelling and get the pus out. Nurses had to hold me down the pain was so bad."

"Didn't they give you anything for the pain?"

"Oh, sure. Morphine. Which, for an addict, was great. The only problem was I had such a tolerance to it from being a user that it didn't touch the pain at first. They added Dilaudid, a morphine derivative, and that helped with the pain, but in the end I was in worse shape."

"Why worse? You got treatment."

"The infection was healed, but now I'd had about twice the amount of drugs I was using before. It was not good. And it was not the fault of the nursing staff. I kept asking for more, more, more—because I was in pain, but also because that is what an addict wants."

"I see."

"You know how [the actor] Phillip Seymour Hoffman died? He was using Ace of Hearts —smack with Fentanyl in it. When I heard about this, I was thinking: if I was still an addict, I'd want some of that. It's part of the more, more, more that every addict wants. That's the thing with heroin—you can never get enough."

At this moment, a realization struck me like a thunderbolt: *This man is not a criminal, he has a disease. A disease that, like any other disease, needs treatment.* But we as a society are stuck in the Middle Ages, when the mentally ill were burned at the stake to drive out possession by the devil.

I said to Jacob, "You must have your lawyer impress upon the court that this thing you are dealing with is no different than an amputated limb or polio. You have a disease. It has changed your brain neurologically.[19] The court would not jail a person with polio or an amputated limb, it would be cruel and unusual punishment. The court must not jail you because you have this disease of substance misuse."[20]

He told me how it all started. The year was 1985. Jacob had flown to Spain to meet his ship at the Rota Naval Station. The first thing his crew members did was initiate him by getting him high on hashish and alcohol on his first day on the ship, an LPH class US war ship—essentially a helicopter carrier.

"Over the course of my stint in the Navy, I was introduced to drugs in every port of call. Once you're out on liberty you just can't wait to cut loose from the regimentation of ship life. Mallorca was the best. You can get whatever you want there!"

Jacob says this with a gleam in his eye, but his body language betrays him. There is a slouch in his posture and a nervous laugh. The way you laugh when you know something is not quite right.

Over the next hour Jacob explained to me the events that led to his being afflicted with Post Traumatic Stress Disorder.

His job on the USS Guam was Damage Investigator. That meant whenever someone or something was hurt or damaged it was Jacob's job to look into causes and submit a report.

He explained that a motor needed to be lifted out of an engine room. To accomplish this, three levels of stairs needed to be cut out of the ship, leaving sharp steel edges exposed.

An over-zealous lieutenant had been conducting excessive drills at night. Personnel from different parts of the ship were ordered into areas they were not familiar with in near total darkness.

Jacob said the lieutenant ordered a squid (in Navy terminology, a new sailor—young and inexperienced) into the construction area. This guy fell three stories onto a jagged piece of steel where the stairs had been cut out, tearing his leg open. Jacob found him while he was bleeding out from his femoral artery. With no medic training and only a flashlight, it was up to him to save this young man's life. After days and nights of grueling work, overtired and sleep-deprived, Jacob said he was scared like never before. But he saved the man's life.

No report was filed. The XO (executive officer) and the lieutenant were demoted in rank for driving the crew too hard for no good reason. The squid who fell did survive, but he would never walk right again.

The experience left Jacob with Post Traumatic Stress Disorder. The drugs had started before this terrible incident, but afterwards he became dependent on them just to function with the stress of life on the ship.

Weekend 15

When I arrived on Friday, D-Dorm was full except for one bunk, the least desirable one, right under the giant bank of four buzzing fluorescent bulbs. I also got given an old beat-up sleeping pad which looked like it had all the stuffing knocked out of it.

It was awful. I could not sleep all weekend. By the time I was released on Sunday night, I was walking like a ten-thousand-year-old man. A tightening band of pain was gripping my lower back.

When I arrived home on Sunday, my partner Phoenix could see I was having trouble bending and picking things up—even my socks and shoes. She often helped me to put things into a positive perspective and said: "Let me know if you need me to bend over for you."

I looked at her and we both burst out laughing. It was one of those moments when you either cry or laugh. The comic relief was badly needed to break up the misery I was in. We laughed until we cried.

I said: "Thanks, babe, maybe later! I think I just need a hot bath right now."

This weekend, I spoke some more with Stuart. A deepening trust had begun to develop between us. Then out of nowhere, he says, "The addiction didn't start in the military. I was traumatized way before that."

"What sort of trauma?"

"Not the sort of thing men talk about—I mean come on, we're taught to suck it up and be strong, right? We don't talk about stuff that could bring shame on the family. I was sexually abused when I was four years old."

Given the healing work I have seen Phoenix do at the

Delmar Wellness Center, I am not shocked. I had a sneaking suspicion that some kind of abuse was deeply buried at the heart of Stuart's addiction. I start to well up with emotion. "I'm sorry. How long have you been holding on to this?"

"My whole fucking life."

We are both looking at the floor now. Direct eye contact is out of the question. I can feel the shame Stuart is experiencing. It has taken incredible vulnerability and courage for Stuart to say this. All I can do is hold the space of acceptance, and just be.

After a few minutes, the guard comes into the dorm and breaks the silence by doing his counts.

The area of sexual assault is not one I am very familiar with, but I say to Stuart: "I can see that this has had a profound effect on your life. The very fact that you have had the courage to share it is by itself a powerful act that will begin to decouple the connection between the drugs and the emptiness. There is a new space for love to enter now."

"I never thought I would. About five years ago at an AA meeting, a woman stood up and shared her story. It was similar to mine and she busted open crying. I thought to myself at the time—there's no fucking way I'm going to do that!"

"Yeah, it's really scary to let stuff out where you think you're going to be judged harshly. It feels impossibly vulnerable. But it's the path to healing."

"I never really felt I could talk about it."

I grab a piece of paper and say: "Stuart, I want to tell you my story."

"When I was in kindergarten, we had this art class to make a candle for Christmas. Each child was given a wick and took a turn to dip his wick in into molten wax and gradually, turn by turn, make their candle. However, at some point, I went ahead of the other children because it seemed to me my candle was not formed properly. My teacher, Mrs Ulrich, caught me and put me out in the hallway. That made me feel really angry and I felt unfairly treated—like the punishment was too harsh. I mean WTF! I was five! I didn't know any better!

I draw a circle on the paper and label it "What happened."

Inside the circle, I write: "All that happened was I cut the line and I got put in the hall."

I draw a second circle labeled "My story."

"But what else did I do? I made this experience decide for me that authority figures are mean, nasty and unfair. And I've had a problem with authority my whole life. In fact, my favorite expression is QUESTION AUTHORITY. What is crazy is that this story, which I made up at the age of five, has run a large part of my life."

Stuart looks at the circles. I jump in again: "When you got molested, you made it mean something too. You were too young to grasp it with language because you were only four. But I promise you—you have a memory of it. It is not the kind of memory that you can recall in pictures and words. It's what we call a somatic memory, a kind of knowing that is in your body. It's more like a feeling."

"That's probably why I'm so fucking angry all the time."

"It is definitely worth exploring. There might be a story deep in your psyche that goes: 'I can't trust people, I'm unlovable, I'm scared and I'll never feel safe.' These are just some possible stories. You're going to have to do the work and find out for yourself what exactly you made that event mean. Once you do, you can start to change the narrative. You can use your own words, your own power of creation, to turn the context around."

"Context?"

"Sorry. Context is the environment in which the event takes

place. Like in my situation, getting sent out in the hall meant for me that authority figures are nasty and unfair, right?"

"Yeah."

"Well, in my Landmark Forum, I turned that disempowering context around. I created a new narrative. What if Mrs Ulrich was thinking of the other children? What if she just wanted the candle dipping to be fair for everyone? What if she was trying to teach me fairness, even if the way she did it was clumsy? When I saw it that way, I could forgive her in that moment. And also forgive myself for being a silly little boy who cut the line to get an extra dip on his candle."

I ask Stuart: "Have you forgiven your assailant?"

"Yes."

The speed of his reply takes me aback.

"Really? Do you know who it was?"

"No."

"It might take some time to really get complete with it. My own healing process was years in the making. Phoenix, who was sexually assaulted as a child, told me it took her about twenty years to fully address the effects on her psyche. Something that was really helpful for me (and for her) was body-centered therapy—especially Reiki, but also the Landmark Forum. Once you get complete with what happened in the past, then you can create something new."

Stuart responds: "Yeah. The problem with all these addiction programs I've been in is that they just keep you in the past. You're an addict. You're a sinner. You're sick. It's a system that sets you up to fail, putting all that shit in your head over and over."

I nod. "There is value to acknowledging what has been, but that will only get you so far. Without a powerful future to live into, a future you create, you're just going to get more of the past."

"Well, I'm sick of that shit. Once I'm out of this crap I'm in now, I'm never coming back again." Stuart stands up.

Stuart's structural language—literally standing up—is a powerful indication that he means business. I see for the first time a clear "Declaration of Independence from drugs."

Ⅲ

The court decided that Leslie should do a "Shock Program" at Willard. That's three months of military-style in-your-face intensive "re-programming" to scare people off drugs.

I hope it works, but given what I've seen in terms of the desire to use drugs, there has to be some kind of spiritual intervention. Something positive to address the void that these men are wanting to fill with opiate drugs.

According to Stuart, who has done the Shock Program himself once, it is "designed to fail." It is not a very comprehensive program, it relies too heavily on discipline, and there is not enough emphasis on the root causes of abuse, trauma, anxiety and depression. It is not a substitute for good coaching, counseling, and men mentoring other men.

The new resident in D-Dorm, Jimmy, was picked up in Miami, Florida on a warrant from fleeing New York State on a DWI—Driving While Intoxicated—appearance ticket. He doesn't talk much. He seems pretty pissed off that he's back in NY where it's cold and dark.

DWI enforcement has gotten very draconian in New York and not entirely because there is a huge public safety problem. The state has a huge financial incentive in DWI enforcement now that they have figured out that it's a big money-maker for municipal and state coffers. The average case works out to about $10,000 in fines plus whatever money is at stake for the prison-industrial complex. In New York, there were 25,139 convictions in 2013 for DWI. If you do the math, that's $25 million in revenue.

Given the effects of alcohol on driving ability, I wonder how much more severe things are going to be when marijuana is legalized in New York and surrounding states. One joint (marijuana cigarette) equals about 0.08 of impairment using the alcohol impairment rating system. When alcohol and marijuana are combined, the impairment doesn't double. It triples.[21]

What is most interesting is if you plot DWI deaths against convictions, you find that the public coffers are growing exponentially, but the public benefit in terms of safety is quite small. There are nine million people in New York state and 323 people died in drunk driving accidents. As a comparison, 16,500 people died in New York state in 2008 from the use of prescribed pain medication.[22] These drugs (Vicodin, Oxycontin, Hydrocodone, Oxycodone, and others) are legal. There's virtually no enforcement on the misuse of prescription drugs.[23]

The FDA has just approved Zohydro,[24] a pain medication ten times more powerful than Oxycontin, which poses a risk of death from overdose from as few as two pills.

Do I blame Jimmy for fleeing NY? Yes and no. Yes, because drunk driving is totally unacceptable; no, because, given the stats just cited, he knows he is going to get railroaded into heavy fines and jail time because of the political climate around alcohol addiction.

Where is the outrage over the thousands who have died from prescription medications? How many accidents and deaths have been caused by driving while under the influence of pain medications or other meds that may have mind-altering effects, such as the temporary loss of consciousness that occurs in older adults on prednisone?

Weekend 16

This Friday's entry into the jail was difficult. The back pain I experienced last weekend was still very much with me.

After consideration, I realized a combination of things had led to the pain. It goes without saying that the bunks are medieval, but a secondary factor (something that Phoenix figured out) is that I may have been too open to the pain of the inmates in the jail. Being an empathetic person, I did not shield myself emotionally as I listened to Juan. She thinks the result was that I began to carry that pain in my body unconsciously.

The only other time I have noticed something like this was when I first got into chiropractic. My first year in practice, I used to have terrible pain in my hands and elbows. I discovered quite by happenstance, when discussing the problem with a man who was a clairvoyant, that I was "taking on the pain of my patients." He said that I needed to be careful: it was okay to be concerned and helpful, but not get too involved in my patients' emotional lives—if I did, he said, I would not be effective as a doctor for very long. After that, I kept some distance from the pain that patients were experiencing and my hands and elbows felt better. Since then I've been able to be both concerned with people and free of pain. I think this remembering served me well because on Monday I felt like I was getting better.

An officer stops me as I walk down the hall with my bunk under my arm.

"Let me ask you something. My friend injured his back..." He launches into the whole story.

On Saturday afternoon, after a night of misery, I felt that I had to do yoga. When the dorm emptied out for indoor recreation, I pulled the silly sleeping pad off the bunk, put onto the floor by the door with the draught, and began. It was just Juan, Anton, and me in the dorm. The others were playing ping-pong. Snow and ice in the outside rec yard prevented outdoor activities.

Juan took a seat on his locker and watched as I went through the poses. Lying flat had been painful for me all week, so I started in Corpse pose with my knees up and rolled off to one side. Deep breaths. Five seconds in through the nose, seven seconds out through the mouth. This little trick I learned from Deepak Chopra, as a way to entrain the central nervous system to favor parasympathetic dominance. After five minutes of this, I begin to drop down a level, that is to say, I began to notice my breathing change. My body had begun to de-stress.

With each pose, I speak out loud what I normally would keep to myself. All the mind-chatter that comes up.

"I'm angry about my back. I'm a chiropractor—this shouldn't be!"

"Now that, right there, is just noise I'm talking," I say to Juan. "It is just the machinery of the mind running amok. It has no value other than to be a source of upset. In the world of standards and ideals, there can only be disappointment and the experience of 'never enough.'"

I roll onto the other side.

"These thoughts are like hooks. They grab at you. The trick is to notice them and as soon as you can, let them go. It's like watching a cloud float over the horizon. You see the cloud. You notice the cloud. You may even appreciate it, but you have no attachment to it. You let it float away."

I turn over for Cobra pose. "What shit are they going to feed us for lunch today?" drifts into my head. That's just more noise.

After several more poses, things settle down. The more I focus on my breathing, the less the mind chatter rises to the surface.

At some point between Child pose and Lunge, a message comes to me through my mind noise. I recognize the voice as different from the others. It is neutral but clear, and it feels good to me.

"Juan, I just got something ... I AM! Did you catch that? Exodus 3:14. That's the voice of God. It came through the noise. It is an affirmation of the spirit in me, a declaration of the little piece of God in me, from the God of all things great and small."

"I AM." These two words are so small and yet speak so loudly. They remind me of Walt Whitman's lines:

Oh me! Oh life! of the questions of these recurring,
Of the endless trains of the faithless, of cities fill'd with the foolish,
Of myself forever reproaching myself, (for who more foolish than I, and who more faithless?)
Of eyes that vainly crave the light, of the objects mean, of the struggle ever renew'd,
Of the poor results of all, of the plodding and sordid crowds I see around me,
Of the empty and useless years of the rest, with the rest me intertwined,
The question, O me! so sad, recurring—What good amid these, O me, O life?

Answer.
That you are here—that life exists and identity,
That the powerful play goes on, and you may contribute a verse.

I exist! I AM! It is the first cry from the womb. It is the last breath of the dying trying to hang on to life. It is everything that spans the arc of a human life.

As my routine closes, I ask Juan if he wants to give it a whirl; without hesitation, he jumps right in.

We are two inmates dressed in striped pajamas on thin green mats, doing yoga in a dormitory with a dozen bunk beds, under the glare of harsh fluorescent lights, with corrections officers coming and going. An officer comments: "I'm not even going to ask what you two are doing."

As we go through each pose, mental noise comes up for Juan. As he lies on the floor in Corpse pose, I can feel how tense his body is. I watch his chest rise and fall. His breath is staccato—labored. I put my hand over his heart.

"Try slowing it down a bit," I say, as I massage the acupressure heart point. "When you breathe, take the breath down into your heart. Imagine your heart filling up with love and then exhaling all the hurt."

Juan's eyes are closed but he does smile. I can only imagine the mind chatter over the words I just spoke. At first it seems a bit out of place to do this deep heart-centered work with Juan in the impersonal space of a jail. But if not now, when?

After the first few minutes of feeling a little weird about it, we get into a little bubble of healing and stay there for about half an hour.

"Juan, remember when I told you before that you'd have to do some work to get quiet and listen for the voice of God? Well, this is it. It is not complicated, but it is a practice."

A little while later, when we end our Quaker-Yoga meeting, Juan tells me that he's not sure if it was his mind or God, but he thinks he got a message.

"Really? What was it?"

"Holy and Set Apart ... is what I heard."

"I believe you got your first message. That's it! That's the work!"

"There's more," Juan says shyly.

"Okay. Lay it on me!"

Juan starts laughing.

"What?" I say.

"I saw an eagle with your face on it." He shrugs his shoulders. "What the heck does that mean?"

"Are you familiar with Native American medicine?"

"No."

"In Native American medicine, the eagle represents the Great Spirit. It is the ability to connect to Spirit yet remain in the Earthly realm. I'd trust that message. It looks like I'm your guide for now until you can soar on your own." I laugh because I never thought in a million years I'd find myself in this situation.

Weekend 17

Blake is a good-natured gregarious Black man who stands about six foot one and speaks with a deep baritone voice. My first experience with him was when he woke up Saturday morning complaining that his heart was beating too fast. I overheard him talking to Anton about his sleep.

"Man, I woke up out of a sound sleep last night. My heart was racing like it was gonna jump right outta my chest. I thought I was having a heart attack or something."

"Hey Doc, what's goin' on with my brother here?" Anton asks.

A racing heart could be a number of things. I asked Blake, "Do you suffer from anxiety? Have you ever had thyroid problems? Were you ever diagnosed with an irregular heart beat?"

"When I did my last bid upstate, they found I had hyperthyroid."

"Do you take medication for that?"

"Yeah," Blake says, "but when I got down here they reduced it from two pills to one pill."

"Okay. Did anyone talk to you about your lab results? Do you know your TSH, T3 and T4 levels?"

"No. The doctor just told me I only needed one pill."

"Without seeing your labs, I can't say for sure, but you may need to have the anti-thyroid medication adjusted. When you have too much thyroxine (the hormone that the thyroid produces), it can make your heart race."

Blake is tall and thin as a bean, with two skinny legs and skinny arms. He works out, so his chest is well defined, but his physique matches that of a person with hyperthyroid right down to the slightly bulging eyes.

"When the nurse comes today, tell her about the rapid

heartbeat."

"Okay. I'm glad it's just that cuz it felt like I was gonna die."

"From what I know, I don't think rapid heart rate from too much thyroid hormone can be fatal. It's only happened to you once—if it persists, it should be checked out further."

I asked him, "What are you doing in here?"

"They picked me up on a violation."

"Violation of what?"

"My probation. I slept over a friend's house. We smoked a blunt and my parole officer showed up unannounced at my house the next morning. He made me pee the cup and 'violated' me. Damn! I only had a couple more months to go. Can't a nigger smoke a little weed?" (Apparently not, although it is okay for Uncle Sam to dole out weed to veterans with PTSD.[25])

"Hmm. Three months in jail seems a bit harsh for getting high, but you did know about these random checks, right?"

"Well, sure, but it was a 'wrong place, wrong time' thing. I always tested clean before."

"Why do they have you doing drug testing, anyway?" I ask.

"I was convicted on two drug charges a few years ago. A federal thing."

"Okay. What happened there?"

"I was convicted for being Black, that's what really happened."[26] Blake laughs, but it is an uneasy, deeply sardonic laugh. The kind of laugh that would be funny if it wasn't so tragic.

He explains: "My car broke down and I had to hitchhike. A friend picked me up on Route 23 on his way back to Catskill. Next thing you know, there's cops and sirens and the DEA has me in handcuffs. Next thing I know, I'm being charged with possession and conspiracy to deal drugs and I never even knew there were drugs in the car when he was pulled over. Guilt by association."

I ask him if he felt he got a fair trial. He replies: "The twelve people on my jury were old white people. They hate them niggers. You think that's fair? I got seven years, but was let out in three when my one conviction was overturned on appeal."

I try to sound hopeful: "Well, that was good."

"Good? Are you shittin' me? Them motherfuckers stole three years of my life! And the DA when his ass got beat on appeal comes over to me to shake my hand after he says, 'I'm sorry, but that's how the justice system works'."

"Did you shake his hand?"

"Fuck no. That motherfucker can kiss my black ass! The justice system only works if you're white and you got money. It's a goddam sham."

"Why didn't they overturn both charges?"

"To cover their ass is why. They can let me go and say 'time served on the one charge' and I can't come back at them for unlawful incarceration."

Blake is angry and he has every right to be. Here's a few numbers. In 1946, there were 300,000 people incarcerated in the US. Today there are 2.2 million people incarcerated and another 7 million on probation or parole. It has been called the American Gulag.[27] More people are locked up in the United States than in any other modern industrialized nation on earth.

Ⅲ

On Saturday evening at 7 p.m., CO Rogan calls us out for church. I've never been to the jail church service so I go with Juan just to see what it's like.

I get there and find Owen, the pastor at a local church in Hudson, leading the service. We sing some songs and then

Owen talks about Gideon and the idea that God has given us the spirit of love, peace and a sound mind.

I am astonished: this dovetails beautifully with the work I've been doing with Juan on the practice of peace. Listening for the voice of God and developing the power of discernment for what is of the world and what is divine.

Owen says that he likes the story of creation because it is the story of God's word. I nearly jump out of my seat and want to give my own sermon, because I'm so excited by the synergy of the message. Juan taps me on the shoulder and gives me an all knowing smile. He's getting it in spades too! I'm thrilled.

Afterwards I talk to Owen and share my favorite quote from John 1:1, and he gives me his favorite from Proverbs. "The tongue has the power of life and death, and those who love it will eat its fruit." Proverbs 18:21.

This coincidence of the messages from our yoga practice and the sermon from Owen feels divinely inspired. And it spills out later that day into the rec yard over a discussion of Jesus. It points to a synergy greater than all of us singly. .

On Sunday at 2 p.m., I go down on the floor and start my yoga with Juan again. I'm delighted with his eagerness to learn. Our activity on the floor has a number of observers. One fellow, Arnell (one of the three BBM—big Black men—of D-Dorm) comes over and asks when he can learn yoga. Arnell looks like a linebacker and talks like a badass from the hood. He's the last person I would have thought wanted to learn yoga. It just goes to show—anything, and I mean ANYTHING, can happen when a space of love gets opened up!

Juan's in Warrior pose and I see a guard staring through the glass checking him out. The guard looks curious and respectful at the same time. I'm very proud of Juan at this point because he is not self-conscious at all about doing yoga and getting centered. His actions to get clear are opening up a space of clarity in this place.

After the final meditation in Corpse pose, Juan tells me about another vision that had come to him. He saw himself in a bird cage with an open door. A cross and an eagle were outside.

"Your face is not on the eagle anymore."

"Yes, because you are now driving your own transformation. You see how powerful you are? It only took two sessions to create a future without bars!"

He laughs.

▥

For most of the winter, the inmates have been stuck indoors without the benefit of fresh air or exercise. The effect of this has made everyone very restless. "Stir crazy," the phrase that comes to mind. On Sunday at 11 a.m., the temperature is just about freezing, and the snow has cleared. The guard comes into the dorm and announces: "Anyone for outdoor rec?"

Without hesitation, all 12 of us clamor for the door. I can't quite explain how good it feels to have the sun on your face and fresh air in your lungs when you've been cooped up for hours.

The heating system in the jail never seems to work quite right. I've been in cells on G-Block that have been 50 degrees on cold days. In D-Dorm the temp is always around 80 degrees. Half the time, guys are walking around in their boxer shorts because it's so hot. At times there is a palpable sense of lethargy in the dorm. The feeling of being sapped. A lot of the guys deal with it by sleeping for long periods of time. I wish I could sleep, but my back won't allow it.

I walk in circles with Tor. We talk about plans to build a solar hot water heater. Then I chat with Bigs, a very big Black man, a gentle giant, about the Bible. We debate a point of Christian theology. The issue: When Jesus was in the garden before the centurions came for him, who was he? Was he the son of God in human form, afraid of crucifixion ("Father, if thou be willing, remove this cup from me: nevertheless not my will, but thine, be done." Luke 22:42), or was he the Christ, already going through the holy transformation?

A lively debate for sure. At one point a small circle has gathered for the biblical forensics. I'm no theologian, but it seems to me that the risen Christ was a very different Jesus from the Jesus who had entered the garden. The risen Christ had fully fused with the spirit of God and metamorphosed into a being of light who was defeating death and opening a spiritual path for humanity.

Ⅲ

Anton has been in the Columbia County Jail for over 13 months. He'd been charged for drugs, but hadn't been given a bail hearing. Nor had any trial date been set. The Columbia County DA was running roughshod over the speedy trial rule (section 30:30 of the Criminal Procedure Law). This matter had even gotten the attention of Senator Kirsten Gillibrand, who wrote a letter to the DA asking why the rules were not being followed. This issue of incarceration with no certain date is a violation of habeas corpus and only serves to drive up anger and resentment against the state.

From a purely biological standpoint, incarceration without these controls creates a huge amount of stress on the brain and the body. The criminal justice system should be focused on restorative justice and not just punishment.

The neuroscience of restorative justice[28] shows that people who have committed violent crimes have damage to the part of the amygdala that registers empathy. It is the same part of the brain that registers pleasure (the nucleus accumbens in the case of drug users).

Why are we warehousing criminals in places that addle their brains and make them sicker? Wouldn't it make more sense to establish a system in which individuals could take responsibility for their so-called crimes? I say so-called, because our system of laws metes out punishments for what are merely violations of the sensibilities of the state. Largely, these have more to do with the state collecting money than bringing about a more just society. The state offers no actual rehabilitation.

In a restorative justice system, incarceration would not be merely punitive, but bring balance back to human lives. For example, if you do drugs and get caught, you would be required to have treatment and some kind of community service designed to help you understand the larger import of your actions, namely the effect of drugs on the community, your life, and your family.

Or if you stole my brother's cow, you would have to work out with my brother through a powerful third party (the state) how he will be compensated for his loss and also hear what my brother feels to be a fair way to restore his loss.

These examples are ways to confront the consequences of our actions by including the people we have harmed. But when all crimes are state crimes and individuals are isolated from their communities, the qualities of compassion, empathy and restoration of relationships gets completely removed from the rehabilitation equation.

My back started hurting two weeks go. Only today did I begin to realize that I had taken on some of the "evil shit" Juan said he was involved in, even though he hadn't said what it was.

One thing I am finding out about drugs is that they break

down the forces of will in the spiritual body. Yet it is the will that keeps the integrity of the spiritual body. Without it, any kind of energetic vibration can occupy a person's mind, and I'm sure some of those aberrant energies had got into me. After understanding this, I felt better. I could listen to everything Juan told me, and let it flow off me like water off a duck's back. Ultimately, it is really about developing all of one's consciousness: the thinking, feeling, and willing parts.

Weekend 18

It was 52 degrees outside on Saturday. Inside the jail it was 80 degrees. I find it hard to believe that an institutional facility such as a jail can't manage simple HVAC controls. The problem is not isolated to Columbia County Jail. Recently, a man on Rikers Island, scooped off the streets for being homeless, died from heat stroke when he was locked into a cell that rose to 100 degrees.[29]

We asked that a locked door at the end of the dormitory be opened to let in some fresh air, but we were refused. No reason was given. That door exits to a small area about 8 x 12 which is also locked and fenced on all sides, including the top. Another completely arbitrary and capricious decision on the part of the guards.

By 7:15 a.m., the twelve of us in the room were all sweating and uncomfortable. As for me, I was in a top bunk up by the ceiling and could barely breathe. Sleep was sporadic at best. By the time food was served, I had a pounding headache and my sinuses were dried out.

Bigs is a big Black man standing six feet and weighing in at about 270 pounds. His demeanor is gentle and he's quite soft spoken. I first met him in G-Block when he arrived.

We talk a bit about the prison-industrial-complex. Bigs is absolutely clear that the prison system exists mostly as a tool of domination and control over certain parts of the population. He points to another inmate: "You see Stuart over there?"

A group of guys are playing a heated game of hoop in the yard. "The tall Black dude with a shaved dome."

"Oh, yeah. We spoke in church. He's looking for work when he gets out in a couple of weeks."

"You know why he's in here?"

"No, why?"

"Credit cards."

"What?—he stole people's credit card numbers and bought stuff with them?"

"Yeah. You know what he got for that—six years in jail and 14 years probation."

"That's a long time to be on probation."

"Yeah. You know what else? He's been violated twice by his probation officer. Both times on a mere accusation, without any proof he did anything."

It's now the third time I'm hearing this kind of thing, but I still find it hard to believe that it's common practice.

I say: "Hold on. Do you mean to tell me that if you're on probation, anybody can just call in and accuse you of doing something, and you can then be violated and sent back to jail for six months?"

"That's right."

"I can't believe that! Doesn't the accused have to be given some kind of due process?"

"Look it up, man! I'm telling you that's what happened to him. Hell... go over there and ask him yourself."

When the game breaks off, I approach Stuart and ask him to verify Bigs's account. He does. Word for word.

Bigs and I continue to talk until Whistler blows his whistle to tell us that rec is over. In the interim, we talk about legal process and what he is doing to deal with his own case. Bigs, like the other 19 guys, was swept up in a drug raid. He was in Hudson from New York City visiting his brother. When the cops kicked down the door, he was in the house where his brother stayed, and they found drugs. Guilt by association.

"Bigs, come on. This story is just a little too familiar. You mean to tell me you had nothing to do with drug possession or drug dealing?"

"I knew my brother was into that shit. I just went to see him because he was family. I never dealt drugs. I haven't used drugs since I was arrested at 19 on a weapons charge, when I was in a gang."

"No disrespect, but do you expect me to believe that? I mean, most of the guys in here say they are being charged with crimes that they are innocent of. Or they only admit that they committed lesser offenses."

"I spent seven years upstate. I learned my lesson. I dropped out of the gang, and have not done that shit anymore."

"I heard that you were not charged like the others."

"Yeah, that's cuz I'm pro persona[30] and I'm not copping to dealing drugs when I'm innocent. They are going to have to prove every element of their allegations against me."

I respect Bigs for taking this approach. I know the others plea-bargained their cases down to lesser crimes or smaller sentences. The general feeling around the jail is that if you demand your right to a trial and put the state through the time and money of a prosecution, they are going to throw the book at you. That means they load you up with charges and give you the maximum amount of time for each charge. It's a highly vindictive system. And if you're Black like Bigs, it is even more vindictive.

◫

On Saturday evening, I went to church again with Stuart. I do it mostly to support him. A Pentecostal service is not really my cup of tea. The singing, worship, and out-loud praising of Jesus is a bit much for a quiet Quaker. I stand and hum to the music and respectfully bow my head during the prayers.

One thing I do appreciate is the Bible verses, although I

don't like being preached at. I will ask Owen next time if he'd be willing to arrange the chairs in a circle to bring a little more equanimity to our spiritual gathering, and maybe open up the word of God to a discussion.

My sense is that it is very important to share the Word with the men (and some boys—there are a number in here), but I don't often see any attempt to relate the Bible to their lives. If they could share some of their life stories and be able to map the word of God onto that, it would be a more valuable experience for them.

This week, the verses from the Old and New Testament were:

> And God made the bitter water sweet.
> Exodus 15:22-27

> Come to me, all you that are heavy laden, and I will give you rest.
> Matthew 11:28

In Isaiah, the Jews were brought out of Egypt by Moses and had nothing to drink except bitter water. Moses threw a branch into the brine and made the water sweet.

These are powerful images. I was happy to see Owen drive them home by citing some examples in modern times of the "bitter waters" we have all drunk from.

If not for my daily practice of faith, I'd probably be a mental and spiritual basket case right now. There've been times recently where I've felt like the character Cate Blanchett plays in Woody Allen's film *Blue Jasmine*. After many marital and legal problems, she says to her sister: "There's only so many traumas a person can suffer before they take to the streets and start screaming."

There is a wonderful story about St. John of the Cross (1542–1591). He was jailed for his beliefs and given rotten food and fetid water in prison. He prays over these things and asks for the blessing of God. The legend says he doesn't get sick but is strengthened by the spirit of God.

Sunday afternoon, Juan and I did yoga. Yoga changes the brain, and in a good way. It can repair damage to the amygdala, the part of the brain associated with a number of neuropsychological states, such as anxiety, alcoholism, and drug abuse.[31]

I keep quiet for most of the yoga session, only stepping in to provide a little coaching on form and breathing. To my pleasant surprise, I need to do very little. I'm pleased, because I have been feeling overwhelmed by the heat, the noise, and the confinement. My spirit was longing to be in a quiet place. Being a hermit at this point in my life felt rather appealing. Solitude holds attraction.

At the end of our session, I lie in Corpse pose for a long time. In the dorm, the TV is always on, there is loud talking (Arnell talks at about ninety decibels—either he is hard of hearing or was never heard as a child). There are other sounds too—laughter, the shuffle of feet, the toilet flushing, and the shower running. Yet, with all of this, I am able to shut noise out.

For half an hour, all I can see in my mind's eye is a pair of pursed lips. I wonder about this odd image and then all at once, it hits me that I've done entirely too much thinking and too much talking. It is time to take a rest.

Juan shares his message of freedom. We don't talk about it either. It just is.

Back in November when I got my 26 weekends sentence, I had to inform the company I do consulting work for that I could no longer work on the weekends. Since the information was public knowledge and there was going to be a good chance my war tax resistance would be known, I decided to tell them the truth.

Their response: they fired me.

I applied to the probation department this week to attend a speakers' conference in Las Vegas to jump-start my speaking career. I filled out all the forms and wrote a nice letter.

I got a call about it on Monday from my probation officer. She sounded like she wanted me to have the opportunity to go, but her hands were tied by the bureaucratic nightmare she works in.

"We got your request. I'm sorry, but I'm going to have to deny it."

"Why?"

"It's not up to me." She sounded almost plaintive, as if she was sorry to have to break the news, and hoping to deflect any anger or scorn.

"I knew it was a long shot, but I figured it couldn't hurt to ask."

"You can have your lawyer petition the court and see what the judge says."

"How long will that take?"

"A month."

"The event will be over by then."

"Even if he did say yes, you'd have to petition the bureau of prisons to change the dates for your weekends."

"And how long would that take?"

"A month, maybe two."

"I see."

I was not surprised by the call. But getting fired and losing the income from consulting have been a big blow both financially and emotionally.

And what it meant practically was that I could not pay my tax bill for 2013 for both New York State and Federal Income

Tax. They'd set me up to fail.

As I sat in my office with a dead phone in my hand, I came to the sickening realization that the prison-industrial complex was not some abstract thing that affects other unfortunate people. It was directly impacting my own life. From now on, I will be in a debt spiral to various agencies of government until the day I die.

Chief Justice John Marshall wrote: "The power to tax is the power to destroy." And boy, was he right.

Ⅲ

The week before, I spoke with an old friend, Dick Yarter, about Juan. Dick is a veteran who suffers from PTSD. He informed me that the VA offers programs to veterans in jail who used street drugs to try to deal with the stress and anxiety from PTSD.

He gave me his doctor's name at the VA and I called him. Dr O'Neil told me that the VA has people who are tasked with visiting Vets in prison and doing assessments so that Vets can go to a special drug court.[32]

This seemed like a solution that would work for Juan. I copied and sent the information to Juan so he could discuss it with his lawyer and the Columbia County veteran's representative, Gary Flaherty. I also sent an amicus brief to Juan that lists good reasons why drug treatment is the preferred method of dealing with drug abuse.[33]

Weekend 19

When I arrive in the jail on Friday night, the CO we call Sarge is waiting for me. He has his hands on his hips and is blocking the corridor to the holding area where I change into the silly prison pajamas. In an imposing and authoritarian voice, he says: "We need to talk."

He steps aside and points to a holding cell, motioning for me to enter. He leaves the door open and then sits down on a bench outside the cell—the bench that has the prison "jewelry" bolted to the wood if they want to keep you in one place.

"Did you send a package of DVDs to Anton McKay?"

"I did."

"That's contraband. It's not allowed. Did you think you were going to watch the videos? "

"No, I've already seen them. They were for Anton. I was hungry on Saturday evening last weekend and Anton was kind enough to give me some of his food. I also did not get toothpaste and he offered me some. I wanted to repay the favor."

"You can't do that. Everything has to come from a bookseller."

"I've sent books to myself in here. I really didn't think there was going to be a problem. The dorm has a DVD player, and the videos are like five years old."

"The jail has to buy the videos."

"Can you donate these videos you've confiscated to the jail?"

"The Lieutenant is going to have to decide that."

"Okay. His call."

"Are we going to have a problem with you?"

I don't like his threatening tone. It is exactly this kind of machismo that makes me want to stand up and turn my back on him.

"Can I send letters to the men I've met?" I ask.

"I can't stop you from sending US Mail, but why would you want to do that?"

It's becoming clear that in Sarge's world, the only communication possible between inmates is the kind that involves illegal activity.

"I am supporting Stuart Reddy in his spiritual development. I send him information on the Quaker faith and other uplifting words to raise his spirits."

"Like I said—I can't stop that."

Whistler enters. "We ready here?"

Sarge gets up. Looks at me. Looks at Whistler. "I think we have an understanding."

I get undressed and put on my PJs.

I thought the conversation about the DVDs was going to be the end of it, but it's not. As I march down the hall and am about to walk into at D-Dorm, Whistler motions.

"Nope. Keep moving. You're in E-Block."

Okay, I think, *no problem, a change of place.* This jail is a total dump so it doesn't really matter where I lay my head.

I enter Cell 7 and the toilet is a stinking cesspool of brown. The sink does not drain and there is what looks like undigested food in the sink. It is disgusting.

I'm shocked at the vindictive nature of these guys. In seconds, my rage against the state is front and center. I can feel the blood pounding in my eardrums and I struggle to regain my composure. I close my eyes and recall the words of Pema Chödrön:

> There is nobody on the planet, neither those whom we see as the oppressed nor those whom we see as the oppressor, who doesn't have what it takes to wake up. We all need support

> and encouragement to be aware of what we think, what we say, and what we do. Notice your opinions. If you find yourself becoming aggressive about your opinions, notice that. [...] Cultivating a mind that does not grasp at right and wrong, you will find a fresh state of being.[...] Never give up on yourself. Then you will never give up on others.[34]

I meditate for half an hour and then I'm just exhausted. I unfurl my bedroll and fall asleep.

Next morning, I'm bleary-eyed and every bone in my neck and back aches. Without a proper pillow to support my neck, it ended up being craned all night. The result is a wicked stiff neck. This morning, I'm dealing with a bit of spasm on the left side.

I hear: "Hey! You the doc? Get up. It's time for chow."

I pick the sand out of my eyes and make my way to the door to collect my tray of Rice Krispies, dry toast, coffee and banana. I'm in no mood to talk to anyone, however Max comes over and strikes up a conversation.

In a way, he sort of reminds me of my dad. He's got that same sort of Hell's Kitchen swagger my father has. I get the feeling that Max came up through some shit and made something of his life, as my dad did.

"If you don't mind me asking—what are you doing in here? You seem like an educated man."

He glances down at the book in my hand. "Not everyone comes in with books on the neurobiology of stroke."

I chuckle. "Yeah, I bet that is a rarity."

"They told me you're a doctor. What sort?"

"Chiropractor."

"Ah. And if you don't mind me asking, what landed you in this shit hole?"

"I'm a war protester. I decided not to pay federal taxes, as a protest against the wars in Iraq and Afghanistan."

"Okay!" His face brightens. "I see we have a man of principle here!"

"Yes. This is where principles get you." We both have a good laugh.

Max takes a more serious tone: "All kidding aside, if you don't have principles, what are you? Just another schmuck drifting through life with his head up his ass."

Max has some pretty strong opinions and since I just met him, I'm not going to say anything to cross him. I'm the new guy in town and I don't know the lay of the land yet.

"How about you?" I ask.

"Felony Assault with a deadly weapon. I shot a guy who came on my land with a gun and was shooting at my dog. I spent five years upstate. Now I'm here on a probation violation."

"For what?"

"I've been accused of assaulting a guy who owed me money. I 'illegally' (he uses his fingers to show quotation marks) entered my own rental property to collect rent which was three months late."

"I'm beginning to get the idea that you're not somebody to mess around with!"

"Let me put it this way. I'm a Jew. My people have been screwed over too many times. Don't fucking steal from me and don't fuck with my family. I loved that dog."

"Did you kill the man you shot at?"

He laughs. "No, I just taught him a lesson. You should have seen the look on his face when I pumped two slugs in his legs. He looked at me holding the gun. He looked at his bloody legs. He looked at me again. And then it finally dawned on him that he fucked with the wrong guy. You think he'll ever come on my land again?"

"This might seem like a stupid question, but if he was on your land with a gun, shooting at your dog—why did they prosecute you instead of him?"

"It's this bullshit New York law called Article 32. In New York, you have an obligation to retreat even if some crazed person is shooting your dog and you've got bullet holes in your house."

"What?"

"Crazy, right? If I was in Texas or Florida, he'd be the one sitting in jail and I'd be with my grandchildren." (The only two places that don't have the so-called Castle Law—a reference to the Middle Ages, a man may protect his castle—are DC and New York State.)[35]

"What would *you* do?" Max wants to know.

"If you're looking for agreement, I think you're asking the wrong person," I respond. "I'm a Quaker. Quakers don't really use violence to solve problems."

"Oh, like the Oatmeal guy?"

"Yup. Quakers believe in non-violence. It's been that way since 1640."

"I never met a Quaker before. So whatta you guys believe?"

"There is no dogma for Quakers like you find in Catholicism or Judaism. The only real rule, if you want to call it that, is that Quakers listen for the word of God in quiet contemplation. There are Bible-based Quakers, like me, and there are others who are not. It's really a big mash-up of people who only have one thing in common—they are listening for the word of God."

"So there's no minister?

"Nope. The meeting as a whole is the clergy. So, for example, if someone gets married, the entire meeting signs the marriage certificate."

"Cool. I like that. Jews are very different. We're all about laws. We've got like six hundred of them. The guys in here think I'm nuts cuz I mumble in my cell with my yarmulke on. The drug addicts in here don't even know what Hebrew sounds like. One guy thought I was a Muslim. How funny is that?"

Then Max wants to know: "Do the guards ever hassle you as a Quaker?"

"No. I don't see why they would. I just sit in my cell with my eyes closed in prayerful meditation."

"They give me and a bunch of Jewish guys upstate all kinds of problems. They wouldn't let us hold Seder or celebrate any of the other high holy days. I remember this one fat fuck up there who was so ignorant—I told him: 'We're having our celebration ... you're gonna have to break it up ... and when you do, I'll sue your stupid ass.' He did. And I did."

"And?"

"The case is pending in Federal Court for the New York State Department of Corrections violating my right to exercise my freedom of religion. I learned an awful lot from those jailhouse lawyers up there."

Max wants to know about my situation: "I'm guessing you have a similar case?"

"Not really," I say. "There is no basis that I know of for suing the government for jailing you for not paying taxes because you don't support war on First Amendment grounds. I believe they were lenient on me, because of my faith and other factors like my cooperation and my family situation."

I ask him: "Why'd you shoot that guy instead of talking it out?"

"You gonna talk when someone is shooting at your dog? Your house? Are you fucking crazy? I did what I was trained to do."

"Excuse me—trained to do?"

"I'm a marine. Once a marine, always a marine."

"Is that how you got that nasty scar on your forearm?"

"Vietnam: 75 clicks north of Saigon on the Mekong River on a night patrol. I was part of a team called the night predators."

"So what happened?"

I got dropped by helo with a team of three guys. There were six teams total along the river at various points. We fanned out about a mile from each other along the river while a recon team was five miles upriver looking for Viet Cong. If they flushed them out, we were supposed to be the mop-up crew."

"So you're walking on the riverbank..."

"No. I'm wading in about three feet of water. There's weeds, I've got a mini flashlight in my mouth, and I can see about two-three feet in front of me. It's pitch black all around. I hear a ripple of water behind me and turn, and before I know it, there's a gook with a machete swinging for me. I raise my arm to protect my neck and he takes muscle, bone, and nerves out of my right forearm. Before he has a chance to go at me again, I swing my M-16 around with my left arm, pull the trigger, and it's over."

"Were you okay?"

"Okay? Hell no. I'm bleeding all over the place and bits of skin and muscle are hanging off my arm."

"Could you call for medical help?"

"No. I've got no radio and it's radio silence until the pick-up point in four hours."

"So you're totally on your own? Did you have any medical supplies?"

"Yes, on my own. I have some Styptic powder in my pack which is supposed to stop bleeding, but I've cut an artery and it's not looking good. I'm losing a lot of blood. I pour the powder on and wrap it the best I can with one hand."

"You must have been in a lot of pain, eh?"

"I never had pain like that in my life. It felt like someone was trying to rip my arm off. We were given morphine in our med-packs and oh, yeah, I took a shot of morphine. Luckily, I was not one of those guys who got hooked on that shit. I smoked a little weed over there, but there were guys who turned into junkies. Lots of guys used the syringes in the med-packs."

"I bet you saw plenty of drug stuff over there."

"On a troop ship on the way home, I was down in stowage smoking with a bunch of guys and we pass by the storage locker for ship's captain. I see this big tarped thing on a palette and I'm curious what's in there. So I pull back the tarp a little and use my jack knife to slit the plastic. Guess what's in there?"

"Do I want to know?"

"A bale of marijuana."

"I'd heard a lot of drugs were smuggled back from Vietnam. I guess that's how they did it."

"That's one way. In coffins was the other."

"So getting back to your injury ... how'd you get out of there?"

"When I don't show at the rendezvous point, my team comes looking for me. By that time, I've lost four and a half quarts of blood and I'm really dizzy and can't stand up. They hump me a mile and a half back to the helo pick-up site."

"Did you ever wonder if you were gonna make it out of there?"

"*No man left behind* is the code of the corp. I knew I'd get out of there, I just wasn't sure if I was going be alive!"

"Where did you go for treatment?"

"First Okinawa and then to Bethesda Naval Hospital."

"How long did it take to get your hand function back?"

"I had like five surgeries and then seven months of grueling daily rehab. They had me squeezing balls and pushing my hand deep into sand and then making a fist. The doctor that put me back together said there was chips of bone missing, shredded tendons, and a bunch of muscle gone."

Max has a zipper tattoo that runs from his elbow to his wrist. It is there to try and make that ugly scar look better. The zipper is open because that wound is still not healed. He has some loss of function in his right arm.

"Max, can I ask you a personal question?"

"Sure."

"Did you suffer from PTSD from that event?"

"For two years, I had bad dreams. I'd wake up in the night thinking I was being attacked."

"How about the shooting business that put you in here? Was any of that a post-traumatic reaction?"

Max looks down. He pauses. Lifts his head and looks me right in the eye. "You can take the marine out of Vietnam, but you can never take the marine out of the man. What can I say? They trained me to shoot when under fire. And now I'm caught up in this Article 32 law."

Ⅲ

The sky is grey and overcast. It's going to rain today. I'm surprised to learn we are called for outdoor rec.

I connect with Stuart and tell him the reason I'm not in D-Dorm. He's surprised at the jail's response.

"What the fuck is wrong with these assholes? I mean it's not cigarettes or pot. There's a DVD in the dorm. DVDs are allowed. They just never get any for us, the cheap bastards."

"It's alright. I'll find another way to donate some films for you guys. Anyhow, listen up: did you get the stuff I sent you?"

"Oh, yeah. The amicus brief and the stuff from the VA on special drug courts for Vets."

"You gonna take action on that?"

"Well, I don't want to step on Gary's toes. He's helping me with the VA."

"Look, you have nothing to lose letting me intercede on your behalf. I'll connect Gary Flaherty, the liaison to the court, and Dr. O'Neil at the VA. Let them work it out. Nobody will feel diminished by having these two men work on your behalf."

"Yeah. I can see that... Okay, you've got the green light."

Stuart gives me his social security number so I can help Dr. O'Neil find him in the VA system.

"You're gonna take care of that number, right?"

"Stuart, do really think I'm going to steal *your identity*? I mean, come on, dude, your credit and criminal history are hardly desirable."

He laughs.

I'm a little pissed off that he even suggested such a thing, but I realize he's not in a position to trust anyone in here. I change my tone.

"Stuart, I deal with sensitive information every day. Patients trust me with the most intimate details of their health, and also give me their credit card information, insurance information, and their social security numbers to file their claims. I'll keep your information safe."

"I'm sorry. That was stupid. I know I can trust you. You've done a lot for me so far."

We discuss some details of how Dr O'Neil can get a person to the jail to assess Stuart.

Then he confides that he had a less than honorable discharge from the Navy.

"What happened?"

"I got caught with drugs in my urine on ship. Back in the day, they did not consider it a medical issue. They dealt with addiction as a discipline issue and they just kicked my ass out."

"Does Gary Flaherty know about this?

"Yes. He doesn't think it's going to be a problem for getting me help from the VA."

I'm a little disappointed that bits and pieces of information come dribbling out like this. I don't quite get why Stuart is not disclosing all the facts to me. Maybe he's not sure I can make any difference. I put the question directly to him: "Do you want me to connect Gary to the VA doc? To facilitate this thing for you? Because I'm getting mixed messages here."

"I just don't know which way to go. Gary's telling me he can get me a treatment program, but no promises. My lawyer's telling me not to fight anything, but rather go with a plea deal that includes a B Felony. And you're in the middle."

"Okay. I get it. But let me ask you this... do you think an assessment by a VA doctor is going to hurt your cause for a drug treatment program?"

"No."

"Do you think if the judge in your case had a bit more information about how the Navy fucked you up, that it would that help you or hurt you?"

"Help me."

"Is there any downside to getting a VA doc to assess you?"

"No."

"So, do you want me to facilitate this?"

"Yes, go ahead. You've got the green light."

Saturday night, I go down for church. This week the reading is Psalm 1: "Blessed is the man that walketh not in the counsel of the ungodly, but his delight is in the law of the Lord."

In talking to Max about Judaism, I was reminded of the 614 laws of the Old Testament. To be a righteous man, one had to obey every single one of these laws. I sat there listening and wondering about today. What is the one law of the new covenant?

I think it can be summed up in one word: Love. The verse that comes to mind for me is Matthew 25:40. How we treat one another is a reflection of how we relate to the divine. "And the King will say, 'I tell you the truth, when you did it to one of the least of these my brothers and sisters, you were doing it to me!'"

Ⅲ

Being Black is not easy in Green County. If you're Black and you're hitchhiking home from a party and it starts to rain, don't try to take shelter in an abandoned camp. You'll be charged with burglary.

Alan is 47. He should have been charged with trespassing, but instead got burglary in the third degree.

Why? Because when he was found, there was cut-up copper pipe in the building. The police failed to notice that the pipe was new and was ready for installation, not for being carted off. They also failed to notice that Alan had no tools, no transportation, and there was no forced entry. And that the door was open.

I ask him: "Does it bother you at all that you were charged this way? Do you think being Black had anything to do with it? "

"In this racist area, yes. If this were New York City, I'd take it to trial and prove my case. But up here, if you're on trial, you're guilty!"

"That's gotta piss you off."

"How can you be mad at ignorant racist people? I was the stupid one. I should have walked home, gotten wet, and taken my lumps for not getting a ride home with a friend. Now I'm in Rip Van Winkle-land and I'm gonna get two years in jail. I'll do the time and that'll be that. Two years ain't nothing. I got a good 20 years left before my dick stops working. I'm not going to trial and have them stick me with five to seven years—that's for damn sure!"

I can't say I'd be as stoic as Alan about getting sent upstate and being dealt a racist sentence. If I were innocent, I think I'd do whatever I needed to do to vindicate myself. But then again, I'm white: I expect a certain level of fairness. It is a privilege I can demand. A privilege Alan can't count on.

▥

On Saturday night after the lights are dimmed at 10:45 p.m., I stay up to read. I'm on the last few chapters of *Swamplandia!* by Karen Russell. A brilliant young writer, far beyond her years when it comes to understanding screwed-up family dynamics.

I read a line and burst into tears: "When Mom died she had no idea the giant hole she was leaving in our lives."

It hits home so hard. I am weeping because when my own mother died, it was as if the whole family just disintegrated. My mother was the glue that held our family together. Without her, everyone split off into their own world like the wood had dried out and pried itself loose.

I weep for the loss of my mother, the disintegration of the family I grew up in. I long for a simpler time when everything was easier to grasp. When things seemed just less complicated. When people knew how to mend fences.

My mother—God bless her—forgave. She was no saint, but she knew how to forgive, even though it was not perfect.

As the tears stream down my face, I know no amount of crying is going to retrieve my loss of innocence, the loss of my mother, or what has unraveled in my life.

Maybe the vulnerability of tears can also bring about redemption.

WEEKEND 20

This weekend I'm in a different cell. I know most of these guys because I've seen them out in the yard, although I've only spoken to Bigs. I notice that whenever I am placed in an unknown situation, I guard myself and "take myself away." Perhaps that's just a normal human reaction.

In spite of my withdrawal, I'm given a warm welcome. Without asking for anything, Will tosses me a candy from his commissary stash. It might seem like a small thing, but when you understand how these guys have been stripped down to the bare essentials, such a gift is a huge act of generosity.

I stop taking myself away and start listening. That's all I have to give. Maybe in this situation that is enough.

Just before lights out, Bigs comes over to my cell and says: "I know you're a visitor, Doc, but we have a cleaning rotation in the cell block. You just happen to be next. You okay to clean the shower?"

He says it so sweetly and so humbly, I can only reply with "Sure," even though there is a part of me that absolutely wants nothing to do with cleaning a place where eight other people have had their feet.

It's good because it forces me to confront my own principles and values. As a Quaker, I do my best to adhere to SPICE: Spirituality. Peace. Integrity. Community and Equality. Jail is a great equalizer, and every man on this block, whether he be a doctor or a roofer, is now an inmate.

I don't want to clean that shower but as I've given my word, I'll get on my hands and knees and do it well. For that to happen, I'm going to have to set aside my ego and all the shoulds and shouldn'ts that go with it, such as "Doctors don't clean showers!"

The bucket arrives. I hold my nose and get to work.

After the shower is clean, Bigs comes around and thanks me. I think it was a test. I suspect he was trying to see if this guy was all talk or not. I stand outside his cell and ask him about his life.

My back is killing me after another night on the torture rack.

"Hey Bigs, how'd you get two mattresses?"

"My back is all messed up."

"What happened to you?"

"I got shot seven times—when I was living in New York City and was involved in gang shit."

"Seven times, and you're here to talk about it? You're one lucky dude."

"Lucky and stupid too. Pride and peer pressure got me shot."

"How's that?"

"One of my boys got into a fight with another gang member and I took his side in it. This other dude, who I had no hassle with, took the side of the other kid. One thing led to another and before you know it, we're in a big argument about something we had nothing to do with. Things escalated."

"Fight?"

"No, words. Just a big pissing match. Then he pulls out a .22 and shoots me seven times. In the back and my pelvis. Good thing I'm big because I'd probably be dead."

"Did the cops get him?"

"Oh yeah, he's in Rikers Island and will be for a long time. It's a good thing too because back then I'd be gunning for him after I got out of the hospital."

"After you got shot, were you scared?"

"No, I wasn't scared. I had kinda figured I'd get shot one day. I had a gun, and in that lifestyle, that shit goes down every day. I was more scared in the hospital."

"Why?"

"All I remember when they brought me in was getting a CT and then this little Chinese doctor arguing with another doctor."

"What was that about?"

"'You gonna kill him if you operate,' he says. I'm lying there with seven bullet-holes in me, in and out of it because of the pain med and cuz I've lost a lot of blood. The next day I wake up and the little Chinese doc comes in and tells me they left one bullet in my lung because if they tried to take it out, I'd probably get a blood clot and die on the operating table."

"How has that affected your life?"

"I have asthma now. And I'm no longer in a gang."

"Tell me more about the peer pressure and pride. What's that about?"

"It's biblical. The proud man falleth. All that gang shit is about keeping up appearances, protecting your turf, and backing-up your 'homies' even if they've done something really stupid. When I got shot, I didn't even know what the kid in my gang did. I just defended him because he was in my gang. That's what got me shot."

"How old were you then?"

"Twenty. As you get older, you wise up. God opened my eyes. You got to be humble. He'll bring you whatever you need."

There is a quiet pause in the conversation. The gravity of all it lands on me.

"And your back? How is that now?"

"It's all fucked up. I can't stand for very long. The bullet that went into my lung ricocheted around my spine before it went into my lung. It pretty much hurts all the time."

I think about what would have happened to Bigs if that gun had been a .38 or a .45 caliber pistol.

Ⅲ

Lunch is served. Hungarian goulash. This is a mixture of textured soy protein made to look like meat mixed with brown sauce on a bed of elbow macaroni. It's not tasteless, but the taste is—how shall I say?—artificial. It tastes and feels man-made.

Moore asks me what I'm doing in jail. I tell him about being a Quaker and my war tax resistance. I notice he can't fully close his hand and I'm curious about it.

"What's going on with your hand?"

"Construction accident."

"It's looks pretty mangled."

"Yeah. Should have never went to work that day."

"Oh?"

"I was on this roofing job working for this crazy OCD lady in Athens. I call her up and tell her I'm not coming in to work because it's pouring rain. I called my crew off. The job is tarped and we'll just carry on the work when the weather clears. It's too dangerous to be on a roof in the rain anyway. This crazy bitch keeps calling me and complaining about how I should be on the job, blah, blah, blah. I tell her No. Like five times."

"Did she get the message?"

"No, she has the guts to come to my house and knock on the door. I pull on my jeans and come to the door and she tells me she's going to hire someone else if I don't get over there and work in the rain."

"Did you?"

"Well, I've got payroll and like five grand in materials into the job and she's holding the check. If I lose the job, I lose my shirt."

"I see."

"So I get dressed and I go over there and set up a work tent with my chop saw and start cutting boards for the siding above where I flashed the roof for the garage. She's right there talking and complaining. I'm tired. I'm pissed off. It's raining. I feel like I have to listen to this crazy bitch or she's gonna jerk me off when it comes time to pay. I'm cutting my last board and she trips on the cord. The chop saw moves, and my pinky, ring finger, and middle finger go into the saw. There's fucking blood everywhere. I could have killed that bitch right there on the spot."

"How'd you keep your fingers?"

"Westchester Orthopedic Hospital. Eighty thousand dollars and three surgeries later, my hand works, but I still can't close the pinky, and the ring finger has no feeling.

"Did she apologize?"

"No, and to top it off, she doesn't pay me. That's the last time that'll happen. I'd walk right off the job the next time a crazy homeowner tried to tell me how to do my job. I should have known better."

"How could you? It was your first experience with it."

"I guess."

"So what landed you in here?"

"My own success. I couldn't handle the money. I liked the girls, the booze and the coke too much. By the time I was 25 I had a 10-man crew, three trucks and we were doing five roofing jobs at a time. It was too much."

"So it was good money?"

"I was pulling down about three grand a day in the clear."

"I'm in the wrong business!"

"Well, a lot of good it did me. I got caught with 15 grams of coke. In New York, that means you're a dealer even though I never sold the shit to anyone."

"What does that mean for you?"

"It means three to five upstate. And I got kids. That fucking kills me."

The weight of it hits me. In this society, fathers are not afforded the recognition of how important it is for them to be with their children.

"Is your wife looking after them?"

"No, my mother. We're separated. My wife has a drug problem of her own, much worse than mine. She couldn't keep it under control."

"What will you do?"

"When I'm outta here, I'll start my roofing and contracting business again and keep my shit together. I've grown up a lot. This is no kind of life in here!"

After lunch, we're sitting around one of the big stainless steel tables bolted to the floor and I start up a conversation with Quinn. He's a young kid. Nineteen. He has an unusual tattoo on his arm.

"What's that?" I point to the inside of his left forearm.

"That's our tribal tattoo."

I raise my eyebrows because he does not look Native American. In fact, he looks a bit like an Appalachia hillbilly. Quinn has no front teeth and a buzz cut, and lopes around in a bit of an unusual fashion.

"What tribe?"

"Oh, our tribe. My brother made up the design."

The tattoo has three curved lines woven together like woven strands of a leather belt with a diamond on the inside.

"Them three lines are me, my brother, and my sister. We all have the same tattoo."

Quinn and I talk for a bit about his life and he tells me a story of child abuse at home. His father was an alcoholic and he'd drink and knock the kids around.

"When I went to juvie the first time, it was because my father put my head through a fish tank. My brother and I just couldn't take it anymore and we decided to beat the living shit out of him."

Quinn seems pretty angry. It's just below the surface.

"Can I let you in on a little secret?" I ask him.

"Sure, why not."

"You're never going to get your life back, I mean have it really be yours, free of anger and regret, until you forgive your dad."

"Well, that ain't gonna happen. I tried talkin' to him, but after this drug thing and how he treated my wife, I just don't want nothin' to do with him."

"Yeah, I get that. And there is one more piece to it. You don't forgive him for his sake. You do it for you. Forgiving sets you free."

"How can I do that after everything he done?"

"Quinn, don't confuse forgiving with condoning. I'm not saying you have to accept what he did. No father should get drunk and beat their kids. All I'm saying is that you can quit allowing the hate and the anger to have a place inside of you."

Quinn looks down. I think he's going to cry, but he's just so disconnected from his emotions.

I say, "You can't change the past, and you can't forget it. The only thing you can do is make peace with it, so that something new has a place to take up residence." Then I ask him: "What do you want to do with your life?"

He replies, "I want to take care of dogs that's been abused."

He talks about the dogs he's rescued and he softens. I begin to see the hardness that's come from the pain melt away as he talks about the puppies and cats he's looked after.

"Caring for those animals would be a healing experience for you. A positive expression of the love inside of you."

He brightens and shares a story about a stray pitbull he rescued.

"Pitbulls are a misunderstood breed. It's all in how you raise 'em. I want to start a kennel and do some good for these dogs."

I promise to send Quinn a book on the topic.

Ⅲ

At lunch on Sunday, I notice the name Miran on the prison bracelet of a guy sitting across from me. I see he's eating a pork sandwich and I query him.

"Are you Muslim?"

"Yeah, how'd you know?"

"I just took a guess based on your name. But I see you're eating pork."

"Oh well, I'm not one of these fundamentalist Muslims. I'm like a cafeteria Catholic. I just take what I like and leave the rest."

"Fair enough."

"How did you come to be Muslim?" I ask, because he looks like any other American kid minus the goatee.

"My father is Egyptian, but I was born here."

"Lots of changes going on in Egypt. Have you been following the Arab Spring?"

"Yes, big geopolitics happening there. The Americans have manipulated a lot of things there and poured a lot of money in because of Israel. There can't really be any strong states around Israel because the US has so much invested there. The Arab Spring, I think, is really to just create chaos in the region."

"I can see that. What is Egypt like?"

"It's a beautiful country, but poor. The average salary is like two thousand dollars a year."

"Have you been there?"

"Yes, my father has family in Alexandria."

"They had an amazing library in the time of Alexander the Great, but it was destroyed."

"Not any more," Miran says, "they've restored the entire thing. It is amazing. The town is great too. A beautiful Mediterranean seaside resort."

"I've never been to that part of the world. Quite honestly, after all this terrorism crap, and seeing how the US has terrorized the rest of the world, I'd be scared to go in case of retribution against Americans."

"You shouldn't be. Islam means peace. Most Muslims are peace-loving people."

"How about you? I see you have a scar on your nose."

"Oh that. Well, I got into a fight with George over in D-Dorm. He said some things. I said some things and the next thing I know he smashed his forehead into my nose. Things can escalate quickly in here."

"So what's your story?" I ask him.

"I was in a car with some friends and we were stopped in a routine traffic stop. They searched the car. The girl driving was young and she got scared when they told her if she did not get out of the car, they'd tow it. The whole thing was coerced. There was no probable cause to search the car."

"So what happened?"

"They found 15 grams of coke on me."

"I thought Muslims don't drink or do drugs?"

"I said I'm not one of those. We were on our way back from a rave party. Nobody was high or drunk at the time."

"So what happens now for you?"

"Well, I was at Fordham in New York City. I was going for my business degree and when this mess happened, they kicked me out."

"You seem like a smart kid. Smart enough to get into

Fordham."

"I think part of it was just pure racial profiling. The cops saw I had a Muslim name and they were determined to push the limits on everything. My lawyer put in a suppression motion. It's on Friday. If the judge grants it, the charges will be dropped based on an unwarranted search and I'll be out of here."

"How long have you been in here?"

"Seven months."

"And the coke? Where are you at with that now?"

"That chapter is over."

Sunday night. My last stop on the way out the jail is the holding cell. After I change, I have 10 minutes to kill. I see two sorry-looking fellows staring out at me from holding cells one and two.

The one guy has bruises all about his face and his face is swollen. His left eye is nearly swollen shut. The other guy is totally out of it. He can barely form a sentence.

"You a weekender?" the guy with the bruised face asks me.

"Yes. How about you?"

"I got picked up on a heroin charge."

"Forgive me, but you look like shit."

"Yeah, I'm going through withdrawal. I had a 20 bag a day habit."

"Oh, yeah. Tor, a guy I know in here, told me all about withdrawal."

"You know Tor? He's a heroin friend of mine!"

I'm assuming that heroin friend is a person you do drugs with.

"So how are you feeling?"

"I threw up twice before you showed up. I'm on day two of this."

"Is it better on the second day?"

"No, it gets worse until the third day. The pains in my gut are starting to get really bad. Tomorrow is going to be hell."

"Have they given you Soboxone yet?"

"No, they make you wait."

"Yes, I've heard that. It seems like 'cruel and unusual punishment'."

I turn my attention to the other guy. "What happened to you? Fight?"

"I was beat up by the Hudson police."

"By the looks of your face, they did a number on you."

"They said I was resisting arrest."

Based on this guy's face, it looks to me like the police went to town on him with billy clubs.

"Did the cops use too much force?"

He nods. It looks like he's having a hard time opening his mouth. I let him be.

A guard enters. "Olejak! You can go." He hands me my locker key.

Like Maxwell Smart, I pass through the doors to the outside where the world awaits.

Weekend 21

This weekend, I was moved yet again. I seem to be getting the full tour of the Columbia County Jail. This block was actually rather quiet. I was able to rest for the first time since my arrival in the penal colony. And there were only six of us in a block designed for ten. This group was mellow, there was less talking. And much less general noise, including the snoring and farting which had been big annoyances in D-Dorm.

Ⅲ

Dean is a roofer by trade, the business his father had taught him. By his own account, Dean has done "every kind of roof there is—and I'm damn good at it!"

On Saturday, we sat down for the usual breakfast of cereal and dry toast and he opened up about what he was doing in the jail: Grand larceny.

"A friend brought over a computer and asked me to clean out the hard drive. I should have known it was hot when he offered to split the value of it with me. He asked me to do it because I'm good with Macs. As soon as I booted it up, it pinged my location and the cops knocked on my door the very next day."

"Did you tell them you did not steal it?"

"Sure, but that doesn't matter. When you are in possession of a stolen item, the cops assume you are the thief."

When we talked later, I learned that the stolen computer story had another part to it. A few years ago on a roofing job, Dean had fallen two stories off a roof and herniated two discs in his back.

You can probably fill in the blanks by now. He went to his

MD, got pain meds, was never sent for chiropractic or any other bodywork therapy to rehabilitate his back injury. Then he went from Advil, to Naproxen, to Hydrocodone, to Oxycontin and finally to street heroin.

Dean had a 10-bag-a-day habit when he was picked up for the stolen computer. The wipe on the hard drive was in part to support his heroin habit.

Stealing is wrong and his involvement in it was not naïve, but one has to lay part of the blame at the feet of the pharmaceutical industry and the medical doctors who dole out this stuff without making the appropriate referrals.

I pick up the discussion again: "How did you feel doing roofs with a herniated disc on heroin?"

"Like superman!"

"Superman?"

"I could shingle all day for 10 hours and not feel a thing, and 10 bags of heroin costs a lot less than just a few pills of Oxycontin. The problem is that I made good money in roofing—$175K last year—but I spent $90K up my arm."

"How do you feel now?"

"Like shit. My back is killing me, it seems ten times worse than when I first hurt it. It's like everything is coming back."

"That's somatic memory from the injury that was never healed. The drugs just push the pain and the memory below the surface, but the work to heal the injury never got done."

"How would you know?"

"Oh, sorry, I'm a chiropractor. Working with people with your back condition is my stock and trade. These stories are repeated in my office dozens of times a year. The last fellow who got addicted to drugs was a motorcycle patrol officer with Albany PD. He used to arrest people for drug possession and use the drugs himself to deal with a knee injury after his prescription for oxy ran out. It is way more common than you think... Was coming here hard?"

"Hard is nothing. Going through withdrawal is like having your guts torn out. It was my first time. I was puking every hour for days."

"Yeah. I heard it's pretty awful."

"I just want to get out of here. I've never been separated from my son in his life and he's freaking out cuz he doesn't understand why I'm not home."

"I can totally relate to that. I'm divorced. The hardest decision I ever had to make was to leave my wife. She was driving me mad with verbal harassment and I just couldn't take it anymore. The day I left and was separated from my children was a terrible blow to me. I knew it was for them too, but I had to keep my sanity."

"In my case, I did not even know I had a son until he was like two years old. I had a one-night stand with this chick at a party and didn't even know she was pregnant. A friend of mine told me, and I started to see the kid. I knew the moment I laid eyes on him, he was mine. When I found out she was doing drugs, with him in the house, I called the cops and said: 'I'm gonna kill that bitch, you better get over there before I do.' When the cops showed up, there was crack and coke in the house and CPS [child protective services] gave me my son. I didn't even really know he was mine until I did a DNA test."

"So you raised him on your own?"

"My girlfriend and I. She's Italian and comes from a very family-oriented mother and father. She took to my little guy like he was her own. She's been really great. And my mom and dad really stepped in too, looking after him while I was roofing so I could keep working."

"Wow. How old were you when all that happened?"

"Twenty-six. It was like a switch went on in my head that

said, 'You've got a kid now—you've got to man up and deal with this.' So I stopped going out drinking with my friends and doing crazy shit, and came home at night and played with my kid. The back injury didn't happen until last year. He's seven now. It kills me being in here cuz we do all kinds of fun stuff together like snowboarding and four-wheeling."

"What are you facing for the grand larceny?"

"Six months to two years. If I get that, it's gonna suck. I feel like a stupid ass right now. But when you face getting sick on heroin, you'll do pretty much anything to avoid withdrawal. And it's more than that—just feeling okay is never enough—you always want a little more. What really sucks is that this will be with me for the rest of my life. That gnawing need for the shit."

▥

The relapse rate for heroin use is extraordinarily high—somewhere between 40 and 60 percent. Some experts say it can be as high as 71 percent.[36] Methadone and Soboxone clinics are set up to substitute one addiction for another. This is mostly focused on ending the illegal drug trade (the government hates a black market they can't tax). Methadone also reduces burglary, which is a big social problem associated with drug abuse. But it's not a real solution for the addict. The thing that is so disgusting about this revolving drug door, besides how it destroys lives, is that the drug companies created the problem and it is the drug companies that profit from the "legal addiction industry," gaining as they do a customer who is an addict for life and has been labeled as such by the court system. There is something seriously wrong with a system that is designed to profit from the failure of human beings.

Government is far more interested in the rights of

corporations and corporate profits, and the lobbying dollars that come from those profits than protecting people.[37] Real flesh and blood people don't even factor into the equation unless a profit can be turned from them. In the pharma game, the FDA profits from fees to get a drug approved. It is no longer the watchdog agency it used to be, it has been transformed into a drug approval agency.[38]

In the words of Dr David Graham, an FDA insider and whistleblower: "As currently configured, the FDA is not able to adequately protect the American public. It's more interested in protecting the interests of industry. It views industry as its client, and the client is someone whose interest you represent. Unfortunately, that is the way the FDA is currently structured."

Once approved, the drug money pours into corporate, medical and government coffers whether the end user is a legal drug user or an illegal drug abuser. Either way, Big Pharma wins. The government profits from the human warehouse system when people go off the rails.

All rational attempts to rein in this system are shot down.[39] Here's what Assistant Massachusetts Attorney General Jo Ann Shotwell Kaplan had to say about the public health effect of the new Zohydro, an opiate-derived painkiller than can be crushed and snorted: "There was and is a severe public health emergency that caused the governor [Deval Patrick] to react as he did there. [...] We have unprecedented numbers of people dying from heroin overdoses and other opiate overdoses. [...] To add to this marketplace at this time a drug that's especially, unusually, more than any other drug, capable of this kind of abuse and fatality, is a public health issue."

The response by Federal District Court Judge Zobel: "I think that, frankly, the governor is out of line on this."

Ⅲ

Cooper drove a truck for an ice company in Hudson. He was paid a low wage, and for two years was promised a raise that never materialized. The company grew on Cooper's results, bringing in new accounts.

With a small child at home and things getting tight, Cooper made a bad choice and decided to cook the client accounts. He bought two standard receipt books, used one for himself and one for the company, and skimmed the difference. That difference was twelve hundred bucks over three months.

One day, he mistakenly left the wrong receipt book in his truck. It was handed in to the office bookkeeper who noticed that what was delivered and what was paid for was not adding up. The company confronted him and let him go. He offered to pay back the money but nothing got sorted out.

Two days later, employed at a new job running the cooler at an apple farm, the State Police showed up and arrested him for falsifying business records and larceny. No drugs were involved in his turning to crime, just a child at home and the need to provide.

Nobody likes stealing, but if people can't earn a living wage and have to steal to get by, how about a little shared responsibility? Congress beat back a request to raise the minimum wage to a lousy $10.50 an hour. President Obama had to use his executive powers to bump up wages, but he could only perform that hat trick on federal contracts. The rest of us are stuck with low-wage jobs. At $10.50, that's only $420 a week, and that's before state and federal taxes are deducted for social security, etc. Who can live on $21,840?[40] That is just slightly above the poverty line for a family of four.

As I'm walking the yard, a familiar face walks toward me.

"Max, I shared your Vietnam story with my dad," I say. "He loved it. He's a marine too. Korea. Chozen Reservoir 1951."

"Tell your dad Semper Fi."

"Sure thing."

"Did you tell him the bike story?"

"Oh crap. No. I completely forgot that one."

When Max was a kid growing up on the lower east side of Manhattan, a group of boys took his bike. They were a year older and stronger. When he got home, his mother asked where his bike was.

"The boys took it," Max replied.

"Well, go get it, or no dinner," his mother said.

Max marched down the street with anger in his heart and grabbed the bike from one of the boys. When they tried to take it back, he swung the bike wildly in circles, knocking one of the boys over and skinning his arms on the pavement.

"I see you found a way to get your bike," his mother said, as he walked into the house.

Max nodded in silence.

"Sit down and eat."

As we walk around the yard, Max explains the steep education curve to get the COs to understand Judaism and get him the items he needs to celebrate Passover.

"When I put a request in for the kosher grape juice, Matzah, my yarmulke, my books (Talmud and Torah) and tefillin[41], it was initially ignored. These idiots that work in here probably don't even know about the Jewish high holy days."

"Well, I'm fairly well educated, and honestly, I know some of the words and some of the story, but have little understanding of Jewish rituals."

"Passover is about liberation of the Israelis from Egypt. Come on, Doc, everyone has seen *Ben Hur*. It's the greatest story ever told, you'd have to be stupid not to at least know that Jews make a big deal about Passover."

"So, what happened?"

"I put in two more requests that were ignored and then I finally had to tell these knuckleheads that if I don't have my stuff, there is going to be a lawsuit for denying me the right to practice my religion. O'Connor finally gives the request to Lieutenant Markam and he calls me down to talk to him about it. I explain the whole thing and to my surprise, he actually gets interested."

Passover is an important Jewish festival because it commemorates the moment in which ancient Israelites were freed from slavery in Egypt. Today the desire for freedom is no different. It's just that we have a different kind of slavery now. We don't put people in chains and force them into hard labor, but we do have a very carefully constructed debt slavery system in its myriad forms.

The slavers today have people believing they are actually free while all the time yoking them ever more tightly to a money system that keeps them on a chronic churn of acquiring money and paying off debt. The systems are designed with built-in inflation that devalues human labor and reduces the possibility of capital accumulation. This is one reason why there is such an enormous wealth gap. Savings shrink over time and many people are wary of the stock market. They have a feeling that the system is rigged. And it is. There are other ways to work with labor, capital, and property.[42, 43]

Weekend 22

A fresh-faced kid trainee CO entered the holding cell with CO Joel. I call Joel "the Turtle," because he's slow and deliberate and never sticks his neck out.

As usual, I was asked to slip behind the curtain and strip naked; only this time I had two voyeurs, which felt much more creepy. Standing naked and having to spread your ass cheeks before two massively oversized men is disgusting.

The new kid looked like he was about 20. Probably just graduated from Columbia Greene Community College with an associates degree in "Criminal Justice." He's got his game face on, hiding behind the uniform and being schooled in the systems of the jail. He looks sad to me. Every once in a while, he comes on the block to do the punch—the half hourly checks on inmates with a little hand-held scanner. He has a lost look about him, as if he's not sure what he's gotten himself into. There is a deadness about him—well, I suppose it is in all the guards, really. The only thing that seems to animate them is getting into their enforcement role. Most of the guys who work in this place are doing time just like the inmates, except that they get a paycheck and pension.

Ⅲ

Paco is a 40-something Black man who is outwardly fun and easygoing. Down his right arm are a series of tattoos that end on his fist with "FC1." On his back is a tattoo of Jesus in a crown of thorns. I have no idea what to make of this and I make up all kinds of gang meanings about it, but when I finally get curious, he tells me FC1 stands for "Family Comes First" and the Jesus tattoo was done after he was saved.

"Let me show you my family." He takes me to his cell

and shows me a dozen or so pictures of his wife, sons, and daughters. There are a number of pictures with his arms around his children. The universal theme of love and family.

"My sons are with a different mother. That's why they're Black and my daughter is an oreo." He smiles and points to his wife. It is a mixed family. It is clear that love is present in these photos.

"They have your back when you're in here?"

"Hell yeah, we're tight even after I fucked up with this bitch in Coxsackie."

"Bitch?"

"Oh, that's why I'm in here. Long story short—my marriage was rocky and I fooled around. I worked nights, she worked days. We slept in the same bed every night for a few hours, like we were in the same hotel, but checked out, if you get my meaning."

"I can get that."

"One night after work one of my co-workers from the heavy equipment company asked a bunch of us to go out and celebrate with him, it was his birthday. I had a couple of beers, nothing heavy, and this cute bitch is hitting on me all night. She's drinking like the rest of us. I just assumed she was 21, I'd seen her give her ID to the bartender. After the third time, she's wearing me down. We go outside to make out. Next thing I know, I'm fucking this bitch and it feels good."

"Just a one-time thing?"

"No, I can't get enough of her. I go back to the bar after work a bunch of times and we getting it on maybe four or five times. Until the cops show up at my house with an arrest warrant."

"My wife answers the door. It is not a good scene."

"What happened?"

"It turns out this bitch I met in the bar is like 16. The cops want me for raping a teenager even though the whole thing is consensual and she's holding herself out as 21. She's got a fake ID and is in cahoots with the bartender at this place to get her alcohol. It turns out she's on a PINS petition[44] from a court because her mother can't handle her."

I cover my face with my hands. "That sucks."

"Yeah, tell me about it. I got two felonies for drugs on my record already when I was 20-something. I'm gonna get fucked on this."

"Paco, everything aside, you really did not know she was 16? I mean, come on, don't bullshit me!"

"I swear to you on my mother's grave. This chick looked like 21. I kid you not. All the guys I was with thought the same thing."

I'm a little creeped out by the whole story. I know, from having a 14-year-old daughter, that, as girls come of age, some of them can look far older than their years. In this case, the context seems to be decisive. In another venue, other questions might have been asked, but in a bar, way too much was assumed.

"Okay, but what about her holding herself out fraudulently as being 21. In a bar, drinking, and the bartender serving her? How far were you supposed to go to determine her age? How could you have protected yourself?"

"I don't know, man. All I know is that the DA is making a big deal on this and I'm the one he's going to make an example out of."

"And the bar?"

"Get this. The bartender turns out to be 18 and friends with the girl. She helps her get the fake ID and knows this while she's serving her. Nobody says boo to me when she's hitting on me."

"Wait a minute. How is an 18-year-old bartending and serving alcohol?"

"Fucked up, right? But in New York, you can work as a bartender at 18, but you can't drink until you're 21. Like, that is going to work?"

"And how do you know this?"

"The girl's mother is suing the bar for something like $250,000 in a civil suit and all this shit came out in that case."

"Can you use it as a defense in your situation?"

"I can try, but I ain't got $15,000 to hire a crack criminal defense lawyer."

"You know Bigs?"

"Yeah, he's my cousin. We call him Slaughter."

"He told me pride and peer pressure get Black men into trouble."

"He left one out—bitches. Them bitches will fuck you up every time."

"I just don't understand how a kid on a PINS petition, with a mother who can't control her, can get a guy in so much trouble where there's fraud involved."

"I shoulda kept my dick in my pants."

"Okay, that's fine for a married guy. What about a 20-something kid full of testosterone thinking he's going to get lucky meeting a good-looking girl at a bar? It just doesn't seem fair."

"Yeah, well, fair ain't got nothin' to do with it. You got a record, you're fucked in this county. If I was in New York City, this shit would never fly."

"How's your wife handling this? You still married?"

"You know, I'm blessed there. My wife came to me in the jail and said it was just as much her fault as mine for this situation, she'd let the marriage drift just like I did."

"Wow. You've got a good woman there."

"Yeah. She said we're gonna get through this and be stronger because of it."

"You don't know how lucky you are, dude. A criminal charge with jail time coupled with a divorce is brutal. The child support alone is enough to crush you."

"I know. I dealt with this crap too in my twenties with the drugs. I thought I had all that shit behind me. I've been out of trouble for 15 years; I had a good job, and a nice house, and now this!" Paco lays his head on the hard stainless surface of the dorm table and knocks his forehead three times.

I put my arm round his shoulder. "You'll get through this."

When I hear rap music, the only thing I hear is noise, but listening to Paco, I can see that the words and the rhythm and rhyme have deep resonance with him. So I listen. He tells me about Biggy Smalls and Tupac Shakur, the giants of East Coast and West Coast rap, who were both murdered. One thing is clear—the music is about Blacks living under white domination.

Tupac was named after Tupac Amaru, the last indigenous Inca monarch of Peru to be murdered by the Spanish.[45] His mother was a Black Panther member, who was acquitted of more than 150 charges of "conspiracy against the United States government and New York landmarks" in the New York "Panther 21" court case. During his early life, he was also surrounded by people who had committed serious crimes and this likely contributed to the gangsta image portrayed in his music.

Tupac's lyrics (from *White Man'z World*) point to Black men in particular overcoming white oppression.[46]

Biggy Smalls, from a poor family, had a similar upbringing to Tupac surrounded by drugs, crime and the desire to climb the ladder of success. He was smart, as his lyrics show, but sadly it's all about sex, money, and status. Biggy's talent never rose to the occasion to truly raise people's consciousness, as one can see from the lyrics of *Ready To Die*.[47]

In the end, both of these guys died at the hand of assassins. Their music was a self-fulfilling prophecy. They were, as Biggy put it, “ready, ready to die.”

I’m learning to play the game of dominos. The losers have to “wash the dominos” (mix up the game pieces). Paco has coined the term “ceramic underwater technician” to chide the washers. In our game, that’s me. My learning curve is steep. I’m still trying to figure out how to count dominos and lock out my opponent for the final “copy coup” (lock out with two similar tiles as you lay your last piece) and the 100 extra points that go with it.

◫

Dean asked me if I could fix his back this weekend. I told him I was concerned about manipulating the herniated discs in his lower back without an MRI, but I could work on other areas. So I loosened his neck and upper back and we did some yoga.

After half an hour of yoga, Dean says: “This is great. I feel great. My girlfriend does yoga and I always made fun of her. Not anymore. I’m doing this every day in here.”

The great simplicity of yoga focuses the mind and cares for the body. It takes so little to make a contribution to the wellbeing of another.

Joel the Turtle comes in to watch with his young CO in training. He asks him, “You wanna try it?” The kid doesn’t know whether to laugh or get on the mat. He just stands there like a deer in the headlights.

“Make sure the mats are taken care of.” Joel leaves. I appreciate his willingness to let us do this.

“Everything will be treated with respect, thank you.”

At 3:30 p.m. on Sunday afternoon, we get a lockdown count. This is a kind of stocktaking done by the jail to account for all the bodies they have. Everyone on the block has to go to their cell and lock themselves in, closing the bars behind them in staggered unison. One after another the locks clang, clang, clang—all except mine.

"OLEJAK! Lock yourself in."

"I decline. That's your job."

CO Miles goes off on a tear. "Oh, no. My job is to make sure this place is secure. Your job is to do as you're told. You understand that?"

I refuse to answer. His question hangs there as he stands outside my cell. An uncomfortable pause ensues.

"Well?"

I raise an eyebrow and shake my head indicating a "no."

Miles leaves in disgust. His shift is over and he does not seem prepared to push the issue.

I decided from the beginning that I would never voluntarily close the door to my cell. It is a line in the sand for me. Never once since I've been in this shit-hole have I closed a cell door and locked myself in. It is a psychological barrier I cannot cross, because what it would signify to me is that I have become my own jailer, that I have imprisoned myself and am willing to take away my own freedom.

It is possible that I may be punished for this. Maybe even getting locked down for 24 hours. But, following Victor Frankl, I have control over one thing here and that is the choices I make and the boundaries I set in my own mind. I'm not going to submit to shackling myself.

Miles pushes the cell door shut. I sit there and begin my meditation. The image that comes into my mind is the stone rolling from the tomb of Jesus, as depicted in The Gospel of St

Mark.[48]

As I meditate on this image of the risen Christ, I feel a great peace wash over me. I am safe. I am held by something larger than myself. I reach for the cross around my neck and pray for Christ to guide me. It is then that I notice a new knot has appeared in the string that keeps the cross around my neck. I have no idea how it got there. I try to remove the cross and to untie this new knot, but I can't get it off my neck. I mention this to Phoenix when I get home on Sunday night and she tells me that she received a message for me over the weekend.

"What is it?"

"That this knot is a sign that you are now bound closer to the spirit of Christ through your experience."

Without warning, I am overcome with emotion. I cry for a while, and Phoenix holds me.

"The knot also signifies an opening into the realm of spirit."

I understand that this opening is The Spirit of Grace. This is what is making me cry. I am forgiven. My humanity and the humanity of every one of these men is accepted without judgment for what it is. We are under Grace. I think of 2 Corinthians 12:9: "My grace is sufficient for you, for my power is made perfect in weakness."

Blessed is the name of Christ who dwells in me.

Ⅲ

Late Saturday evening, I see Dorian working away at a table, cutting toilet paper into tiny strips and fluffing them up randomly into a poufy ball. Then he colors strips of white paper that are torn into random lengths with colored pencils. I have no idea where he got the colored pencils.

"Whatcha working on?"

"An Easter Basket."

He pulls out a little plastic bowl he keeps in his cell for his morning cereal and assembles the whole thing into a colorful basket complete with a handle made out of part of a hot cereal box he got from commissary. On the table, he arranges the dominos to form the words "Happy Easter" and leaves a note to the Easter Bunny with an arrow pointing to the basket. "Please leave candy here ↓."

In the morning the Easter Basket is gone. Confiscated by the prison guards. The mean-spiritedness of this really gets me. I'd almost rather they punch Dorian in the face for making the Easter Basket than eliminate any trace of it altogether. That would be more honest.

When breakfast arrives, Dorian shuffles around the block looking for the basket. He sees it's been taken. I'm sad for him. This little act of hope shows me he is just a kid at heart. I think of my own children and how for years we'd color eggs and hide chocolate bunnies in the garden.

"Well, so much for a happy Easter," he says in his Eeyore voice.

I touch his heart. "Only you can generate happiness, don't look for it on the outside."

Dorian is depressed. He simply needs love. I don't know his back story except that he's in some deep trouble and is facing a decade or more in a maximum-security prison. I just want to scoop him up and put him in a situation where there are some strong men around him that can guide him and give him the male-bonding love he so desperately needs.

Weekend 23

Juan had his day in court. Now he has to choose between drug court and a 'bid' (a stint in state prison). As we strolled in our circular walk around the yard, he explained his options:

"I can do 90 days in Willard and then be on a tight leash in drug court for the next seven years, or do a straight two-year bid upstate with two years probation."

"What's your sense?"

"Joe, I don't know if I can manage not fucking up for seven years."

"What does your gut say?"

"Drug court. But all these guys in here say I'm going to fail."

"Listen, forget what these guys say. Most of them can't wait to get out and use drugs again. But that isn't you. You told me you were done with all that shit. What's your word in the matter?"

"Oh, there's that word 'word' again."

"It all comes down to just one thing, Juan. Walk the talk. And only you have the say-so in this matter."

"Well, I told you I'm going to stay clean this time."

"Given that is your word, what's your decision?"

"Drug court."

"The drug court can support you in having the life you want, free of all the drug shit. They could actually be your ally in this."

"Yeah, most of these guys hate drug court coz they want to use again—that's not me. I've changed."

"A man has nothing more powerful than to honor his own words."

"Sometimes I'm not sure."

"So get quiet. Use the tools you have. The yoga. Get centered and ask for an answer. It's already there. You just need to listen for it."

"Yeah, but there's no peace in here."

"You can bring the peace with you wherever you are. The loud TV, the guys joking about you on the yoga mat, the interruptions of the guards—it's all part of it. You are the possibility of peace everywhere and with everyone. Why? Because you say so!"

I have the letters W-O-R-D written across the four knuckles of my left hand. I put it there as a joke when Phoenix and I were discussing the power of word in our Wicked Rich Partnership meeting Friday morning.

Juan says: "The guys make fun of me when I do yoga. They just needle me all the time."

"It's confronting for them. They're going to have to deal with the storm inside of them. But that's their affair, not yours."

The guard bangs the big brass key against the metal fence post and starts calling out: "D-Dorm. E-Block. F-Block." I hear my spot and his voice fades away.

"That's me. Don't forget what I said. See you in church tonight."

Cooper is a new person in the dorm this weekend. I introduce myself and ask about his life. He tells me his story.

"When I was 10 my father remarried, and suddenly I had two older brothers. That was a big change. It was like I suddenly disappeared. I was the little kid."

"I bet that was hard."

"I had my first job when I was 12. I worked at a local farm putting up hay in the summer. I grew up fast."

"Did you decide anything about that?"

"What do you mean?"

"I mean in your kid brain—when all this change happened—did you make it mean anything? Like you're no good, or not good enough. Stuff like that?"

"I don't think so."

"I'll tell you what happened to me. I was ten and I liked a girl on my street, New York Avenue in Huntington Station, Long Island. Her name was Lisa Berger. She was Jewish. I remember it as if it were yesterday. She had patent leather shoes and a cute little dress with short sleeves and it was a peach color. She wore a red ribbon in her hair. She was very shy, I don't think she ever spoke a word to me. I wanted to play with her on the block, but her mother said no. I made that mean I wasn't good enough. It turns out her mother survived the Nazis and the family never let Lisa out of their sight. They were just terrified of something bad happening again."

Cooper responds: "If I had to say something about that time, it would be that I wasn't important and that I was stupid. That was the year the school kept me behind and put me in the stupid kids' class cuz I was getting into trouble all the time."

"Why?"

He gives a sheepish smile, "I think I just wanted attention."

"Yes. I have that one too. I threw a desk through a glass window once for attention. And I got lots of attention. Only it was the wrong kind."

"Well, maybe that's my problem."

"It's all a question of context."

"What the hell does that mean—you're either stupid or you're not."

"Maybe. You've told me that you're good with your hands, right? You can fix just about anything."

"Yeah, so what?"

"Well, I'm good at biochemistry and physiology, but I can't fix an engine. Have you heard about auditory, visual, and kinesthetic learners?"

"No."

"So there are different kinds of intelligence. You don't come across as stupid to me. You have intelligence in your hands. If you honor that, you can rewrite that sentence you gave yourself at 10."

Tor's brother showed up in F-Block on Saturday afternoon on a probation violation. When I found out who he was, I got really sad. I looked at him and Tor talking, and it all seemed so hopeless, as if this family dynamic of swinging in and out of jail was somehow normal. The familiarity of it between them, the easy back and forth of it—that is what made me sad.

Ⅲ

CJ was camping in the Catskills and drove a mile and a half to get some beer at a Stewarts when he was pulled over. It was his fifth Driving While Intoxicated offense since 1979. He told me that when he got his first DWI, you just got an appearance ticket, now you go to jail.

What I found interesting about CJ's situation is that at no point did he (or the state) require he join AA or take some positive steps to deal with the issue. It has been punishment only, straight down the line.

For DWI #4, he spent two years in the Buffalo Corrections Center and did a "Shock and Awe Program" which seems to have been completely ineffective.

My friend Dick, who has been in AA since he was 50, and has remained sober, told me that in his experience, "There can be no sobriety without God. There is nothing but God that can fill the spiritual vacuum that gets created when addiction is present."

What my experience in the Quaker Meeting has shown me is that when two or more are gathered in community to listen for the movement of spirit, something new develops that the individual cannot provide on their own. It is possible to sit anywhere and meditate or contemplate upon God, but when 30 people bring their intention and the peace they have cultivated to a Quaker Meeting House, it is a transformative experience that goes far beyond the short term satisfactions of addiction.

If there is an American addiction, it is the addiction to the notion of rugged individuality: the Marlboro Man riding off into the sunset, well satisfied, with a cigarette dangling from his lower lip. Well, he died of cancer.

We can do some things on our own, but there are some things that are just better solved in community. Addiction is one of them. Without community, the sense of belonging and groundedness, we don't understand what it means to be cared for. Romantic love and the nuclear family is not enough.

We fill the void with useless substitutions for spiritual connection that only delay the pain of loss and the absence of community caring. Sometimes the road is short and can end in an early death, as happened to Phillip Seymour Hoffman or Peaches Geldof, both found dead with a needle in their arm.

Ⅲ

I'm sitting around with Dean talking about the things we love. I talk about my love for sailing. Dean shares his love of snowboarding. And going to music festivals.

"What do you love about music festivals?"

"I love the music, I love reconnecting with my friends, and I love the feeling when I'm there and I'm high."

"I've never done that. I was not a Deadhead or a Phish

follower. The one Phish concert I went to was at the Palace. I thought I was getting good tickets being down front, but honestly it was disgusting. The place was filled with marijuana smoke and the first six rows were turned into a mosh pit."

"Oh … too bad. You should check out an outdoor festival. You might dig it."

"Like Mountain Jam?"

"That's a great one. Last year we went there with bags of Molly and three tanks."

"Molly? Tanks of what?"

"Molly, you know, Ecstasy. The tanks are nitrous oxide, laughing gas."

"I'm not going to ask where you get the Molly from, but the laughing gas? Don't you have to be a dentist to get that?"

"No, I just put a DBA together for distributing the stuff and they give it to you, no questions asked."

"Is that a big thing at festivals?"

"It's huge! They call it Hippy Crack. I get three tanks for $75 apiece and sell balloons of Nitrous for $10 each. It's like $2500 profit on each tank. We'll drain a tank in like ten minutes at a festival but you have to be careful."

"Why? People get hurt?"

"No, the shit is perfectly safe.[49] The problem is the Nitrous Mafia."

"The who?"

"This shit is so profitable that guys have carved out turf for selling it. Once at a festival in Michigan, we had three tanks and were selling balloons and these thugs came out of nowhere and held me down and threatened to kill me with a hand-held sledgehammer to my head if we didn't clear out."

"Scary stuff."

"Fuck yeah. After that we built an elaborate method to conceal the tanks after we went to the festivals. It was a box disguised to look like a stereo subwoofer in the back of the car."

"Did anyone catch on?"

"Nope."

"And is it illegal to sell Nitrous?"

"I don't think there's much regulation on it."[50]

"What about Molly?"

"We don't sell that. We just use it for ourselves."

"I heard that it can drain serotonin from your brain."[51]

"I don't use it very often. Only when we party at the music festivals."

I spoke to Dean some more, trying to understand why this way of life was so attractive to him. It became clear that he was trying to recapture what he called his "stolen youth." I assume he meant that because he had to buck up and be a single dad so early in his life, the music festivals and the drugs were a chance for him to have fun and enjoy life without the tethers of responsibility: one or two weeks out of the year when he could be 18 again.

The long-term side effects on the brain are very underestimated by rave/music festival enthusiasts. The brain damage is small each time you do MDMA or nitrous oxide, but the cumulative effect of being stoned for a week or two on this stuff is not good. Some authors have found that chronic MDMA use causes neuron degeneration.[52] In short, it makes you stupid.

❧

I asked Dorian if he'd ever found his Easter Basket. The answer was no. I told him that an Easter Bunny with big floppy ears and curls had offered him some Easter candy.

There was no way to get the candy into the jail, but we figured out a way: the jail commissary. It was possible to get candy through the commissary, so I got Dorian's inmate number and deposited some money into his account from the Easter Bunny. He smiled like a little kid.

I learned his story as we walked around the yard on Sunday afternoon. Dorian was a kid with a drug habit. He dropped out of school in the first quarter of twelfth grade and went to work at the McDonald's in Cairo as a line cook for minimum wage. A wage which neither affords a life nor a drug habit.

"So what's a young kid like you doing in jail?"

"I robbed a McDonalds," he says matter-of-factly.

"Was it worth it?"

"It was at the time," he says with a smirk. Dorian has a side of him that is full of mischief and a devil-may-care attitude when it comes to matters that others feel are important.

"What did you get out of it?"

"Five thousand two hundred and three cents."

"What'd you use it for?"

"I took a trip to New York City, bought a bunch of pills, and then went to Jersey, bought some new clothes, and just lived a little. I like getting all fucked up."

"Uh huh." I'm a bit at a loss for words because it is hard for me to understand such lack of purpose.

"Did you expect to get caught?"

"We had a plan. I was foolin' around with the cashier. She and I and the fry cook decided to rob the place and say it was a hold up. When the cops questioned each of us separately, our stories didn't match up. To get out of trouble, the cashier and the fry cook ended up blaming it on me. But even though I stole the money, we did split it."

"Did they get any jail time?"

"No, they threw me under the bus, even told the cops I had

pipe bombs and I was going to do some crazy shit if the cops came after me."

"Did you?"

"No, all of that was bullshit."

"So, what do you expect when you get sentenced?"

"Two years with two to four years probation. It's not a lot." Dorian seems to have a rather cavalier attitude about it.

CJ chimes in: "He's going to get a rude awakening when he gets downstate. It's no cakewalk in the New York prison system."

Dorian takes his cup, scoops water out of his toilet bowl, and splashes CJ with it.

"Try that shit upstate, kid, and you're going to find out fast who's in charge."

"Ooooo. I'm scared."

"You should be. When I went up, guys would disappear for days and come out roughed up with a whole different attitude. They called it 'getting erased' when you disappeared for a while. The state of New York owns your ass, boy, and they'll fuck you up if they want to."

Dorian thinks about this for a bit and wipes up the floor.

Weekend 24

For the six months of my faithful attendance at the Columbia County Jail, my back has been a problem. Not just while in jail on the weekends, but also bending at work and small actions like picking up my nine-year-old when she falls asleep on the sofa.

This weekend, I decided to carry out an experiment on myself with Kava (Piper methisticum), an herb known to Pacific Islanders for a thousand years as a central nervous system relaxant and muscle relaxant.

The problem I've been dealing with is not so much spasm, but sacro-iliac joint pain. I've tried a number of healing modalities (chiropractic, massage, and reiki), which have been enormously helpful, but never tried an herbal solution. This Friday I took eight Kava: two at 5 p.m. with dinner and another six at 6 p.m. The net effect of this higher dose regime was a really big relaxation effect on both the muscles and the mind.[53, 54] I actually slept through the night.

New accommodation again this weekend. This time it is H-Block. A very different experience from F-Block. Of course, I made up all sorts of theories about this, like "they're messing with me, just when I get comfortable with a group of guys, they move me" and "they're still punishing me for the DVD incident."

The guys in H-block have been the most closed-off that I'd yet experienced. I could barely connect with any of them. Even so, when I entered my cell, #8, what I found there gave me hope. The last inmate left a heart made out of the cardboard packaging from a bar of soap. He also left the toilet full of torn up paper, which I had to fish out before I could use the facilities.

As I washed my hands, I noticed a little scribble between the cinder block joints on the wall below the polished steel mirror. I immediately recognized it. It was two lines from a song: Oh, such a perfect day/You just keep me hanging on.[55]

The lines came from a song I knew well: "Perfect Day" by Lou Reed.[56] I replayed the lyrics and melody in my head all day, which brought me such pleasure.

I speculated about why the last person had left this wonderful gift for me to find. I had always enjoyed the ambiguity in this song, the pleasure of the other person's company mixed with the sad feeling of being short-changed, and then the prophetic warning in the last lines, repeating four times "You're going to reap just what you sow".

One of the blessings of being in jail is that the empty time allows for more contemplation and reflection than in busy daily life. A lot happens in the quiet spaces when the men are alone, even though not much of it gets shared and there isn't much non-judgmental listening going on.

Perhaps the Quakers who set up the penitentiary system over 150 years ago in Eastern Pennsylvania had a few useful ideas.[57] Quiet contemplation is useful, but of course not if it is overdone and pushes people into sensory deprivation.

I took a book on Haiku in with me about four months ago and never actually got to read it. I found it at the bottom of my pile. It inspired me to write a few haikus of my own:

Sunday Morning
Lights on, cell door opens.
Clang! Eighteen hours to freedom.

Through the D-Dorm window
Two sparrows perch on the fence
One flies, the other stays.

April rains fall
The Hudson River swells its banks
New life on the shore

The food we get to eat on the weekends is pretzels and marshmallows, a sandwich made with some processed meat-like substance, a little cucumber salad and a glass of milk. Not at all appetizing and hardly filling.

What most of the inmates do is use their commissary to fill the gap of hunger that happens around 8:30 p.m. A common recipe I've seen in the dorms looks like this:

Commissary Bowl
1 pkt Ramen Noodles
1 pkt Spanish rice
1 Slim Jim or sausage meat
1 bag of Dorito chips
1 bag of Cheetos chips
Crush up noodles and chips and create layers of noodles, rice and chips.
Garnish top with slices of Slim Jim, add hot water from tap.

Because there is nothing fresh that can spoil, and nothing nutritious, the commissary bowl offers a filling meal with none of the benefits of real food. In fact, this concoction will kill you if you tried to live on it.[58] Bon appétit anyway!

On Saturday morning at 10:15 a.m., a bunch of guys were laughing over a silly news item on TV. Their voices woke up Nash. Just like a bear out of winter hibernation, he was in a bad mood and started yelling and screaming.

"How many fucking times do I have tell you assholes I sleep after breakfast?" Nash shuts off the TV and marches around, yelling at people on the block.

Nash gets to me and I speak up: "Hey, dude, don't speak disrespectfully to me. Whatever is not working, we can work out."

He steps toward me like a boxer steps when he's about to throw a punch. I don't back down.

"Who the fuck are you? You're new here and now you're telling me how it's going to go. Fuck you. Asshole."

"If it's sleep you're wanting, cooperation is going to go a lot farther than threats."

"Shut the fuck up." Nash walks back into his cell, closes his door and lies down. An hour later, he comes out and apologizes to me for his outburst. I say to him: "There's no need to get upset. These guys don't want a fight on the block, and you want to sleep. Talk to them and work it out."

Nash opens up a little. He's from Jersey. Italian tough guy with a bull's horn tattooed on his arm and the twin towers on the other. He could have wiped the block with my scrawny little body.

Nash is in on a DWI. He and Paco share one thing in common— that comment Paco made about "them bitches." He was chasing a 24-year-old young woman in Albany. He was drinking and blew a .08 on the breathalyser the way home to Catskill. Tinted windows got him pulled over.

Now he's in for eight months. "I think I'm done running around. I'm getting too old for this shit. I got divorced about four years ago and I'm thinking about getting back with my old lady. I've had a chance to run around, do drugs, and it's not what it's cracked up to be."

"So what next?"

"I'm going to go back to Jersey and get back in the construction business with my brother. We have a good business down there. My daughter is 12 and she really deserves her father around."

"That sounds like a good plan."

"Well, it's a hell of a lot better plan that doing drugs and doing time in jail."

"I thought you were in on a DWI?"

"Well that was my first offence. But then I got caught with dope. Selling marijuana. I'll be honest with you—I was a shitty drug dealer. I got caught doing it after only three months."

"What started you doing that?"

"I was out of work. I had bills to pay. I knew I could get the stuff easy in Jersey and sell it up here."

Nash goes back to cooking his supper. He points to the bologna. "You know I could never get used to this shit."

"I don't blame you. I've never eaten it the whole time I've been in here. Just the smell of it makes me want to puke."

Tor had rolled through a yellow traffic signal. That was enough for the Hudson police. Without so much as asking to see his license and registration, he was dragged from his vehicle, frisked, and had his car searched without probable cause and without a warrant.

The fruits of this illegal search were 25 empty bags that had contained heroin. If the cops find so many empty heroin bags in your car, you are automatically labelled a dealer. Tor's public defender made no attempt to quash the evidence from the illegal search, and the evidence was used. If you have a heroin habit and use 10 bags a day, which is not uncommon, it is entirely possible that 25 bags could easily accumulate.

A good lawyer might have had knowhow to file a motion to quash. But I've been told by some of the men inside the jail that a "good lawyer" wants $15,000 upfront in a criminal case. Tor spent seven months in jail after he was denied bail—there is no bail for repeat offenders, and he'd already had the drunk driving offense.

The NYS Police Lab determined that there was not enough evidence to hold him, and he was released on his own recognisance after the charge of felony possession of a controlled substance was dropped. He will likely be charged with misdemeanor possession and given time served.

Does it really take seven months to weigh something?

And once they weigh it, if you don't have the cash for an independent lab analysis, how can you be sure the state is doing their job right?[59] It's not like the TV show CSI, where they get it right every time.

The great news is that Phoenix has invited Tor to session #10 of the Landmark Integrity Seminar and he is a "yes" for taking a look at how the distinctions of the Landmark Forum can support him in his life.

◫

Don came into the block late on Saturday night around 10:30 p.m. I walked over and offered him a book and the newspaper. He told me he was picked up on a bench warrant for failing to appear in court for a charge of having prescription painkillers without a prescription.

Just before being brought to jail, Don's physician told him he had a mass on his kidney. The doctor was not sure what it was and wanted a CT or an MRI to determine if it was a cyst or a tumour.

I asked Don if the prison doctor had seen him, he said yes.

He told the prison doctor what his physician had said, but the only treatment he was offered was a gallon of Gatorade.

It is not uncommon for months to go by in jail before medical problems get addressed. If Don has an aggressive tumour, that time lag could mean death. There's no particular urgency if you're "just some scumbag off the street," as Don described himself.

Being sick in prison is no picnic. Lynne Stewart, the activist lawyer who was recently given compassionate release due to cancer, got the worst possible cancer care in prison.[60] Due to negligence, they were killing her.[61]

Don looks extremely dishevelled, like a homeless man, although how you look doesn't matter. If you're behind bars, you're automatically a "scumbag" as far as the COs are concerned.

◫

When we spun around the yard on Saturday morning, Juan updated me about his case. His lawyer told him to plead guilty to the drug sale charge, which would most likely get drug court. This would mean 90 days of "shock treatment" in Willard followed by close supervision under the auspices of the drug court—random urine checks, and a parole officer snooping around your life for five to seven years.

However, it didn't happen. The veteran's liaison to the court had suggested drug court. Gwen, the social worker who has the case, had suggested drug court, and the public defender (Mike Cozzolino) had requested drug court. But no drug court was offered. It was because the DA's office made a public statement in the *Register Star* that "everyone who was arrested in the big Hudson drug raid in December will be dealt with in a group and no deals will be made". Isn't collective punishment illegal?

Juan was moved to a different judge and the drug court option was yanked, leaving him with a possible two-to-twelve-year sentence.

I'm going to write a letter on Juan's behalf, but, regardless of what happens to him, I have been guided by spirit to stay in communication with this man.

There is a total disconnect between what the people of this country want and what laws actually get passed. The US is an oligarchy[62] and that fact is reflected in the high numbers of poor people in prison. High salaried bankers and hedge fund managers never see the inside of a prison cell, even after destroying the economy.

WEEKEND 25

This week it was I-Block. That leaves only one area that I have *not* visited.

My friend Peter Barus says the jailers are moving me to bring transformation to different areas of the prison. I may be cynical, but I think they have other reasons for moving me around.

My new cell has three symbols on the wall: a swastika, a Nazi SS symbol, and the Iron Cross. A very different experience from last week with the cardboard heart and Lou Reed.

One of the guys on my new block, a young headstrong white kid, said he "hates niggers."

"That's too bad," I said, "because 99.5 percent of your DNA is African, which makes you about as Black as those niggers you hate so much."

"Well..."

"Well, it ain't 1962 and it ain't Alabama, and the Klan ain't in power no more. These are different times now. You should take a second look at those racist attitudes you got... Blacks are no different than you and me."

Wayne is a logger who lives over in Sheffield MA. He's in on a parole violation. Yes, the same revolving door that keeps corporate jailers in business! I'd say about one third to one half of all the people I've spoken to in jail are in for their second, third, or fourth term, all because of some minor violation of their terms of parole. It reminds me of the Treaty of Versailles: let's make the conditions so onerous for success that you literally have to break the law to succeed.

I strike up a conversion with Wayne. "My best friend lives over in Sheffield. You know Morvin Allen?"

"Oh, Morvin, hell yes. He's a hard workin' man."

"Yeah, tell me about it. Up at 4 a.m. to milk, and everything else it takes to keep that farm going."

"I knew him when he first came over and started the farm in Alford, Massachusetts. We paved a silage bunker for him."

"I remember that farm well. Shortly after he got there, they had a huge wedding party for him and Gail in the loft of the big white barn. That was a great party!"

After that exchange, things warmed up considerably. What I first thought was a rather frosty conversational environment turned out to be warm and open. You just never know. Whenever I'm put in a new place in the jail, I try not to make any assumptions, because more often than not, they turn out to be wrong. Most of these men are no different than I am. I've only met one guy in jail who I could not relate to and would be wary to engage with.

ADM has a gigantic milling operation on the Hudson River by Hudson, New York. All the flour that makes its way to Price Chopper, Hannaford, Freihoffer's and other bakeries comes from there. ADM—Archer Daniels Midland Corp—a Fortune 500 company, has a lock on grain sales in many parts of the world. Their slogan, "Resourceful by Nature," certainly fits, although a more apt moniker would be "Price Fixing is What We Do Best."[63, 64] Before he was sentenced, Len worked there for long hours at a job that was full of shit work and lots of risk. He got $20 an hour. Given his workload and the dangers, he really ought to have got $30. Not too long ago, a guy at ADM got his arm taken off when a three-ton roller started up while he was clearing out something stuck in it.

Larry says to me: "I just want to be able to go home, do some heroin, do a little pot, and relax in my own home. What the fuck is wrong with that? I ain't hurtin' nobody, I ain't selling drugs to kids. This shit should be legal, just like tobacco or alcohol."

"What if you kill someone at work when you're high? Press the wrong button, or start a machine when a guy is inside it?"

"I don't use when I'm at work..."

"But you are high when you're there, right? Otherwise you'd be going through withdrawal."

"Just because you're on heroin doesn't mean you're fucked up and can't work right."

"Okay, maybe, but I think I can say with some certainty that you are not as fully aware as you would be without the heroin."

"Er..."

"It's okay. Is that accurate?"

"Yeah. It takes the edge off. I'm less annoyed about all the shit I have to deal with at work. Like the assholes I have to work with."

"So what's it like there?"

"It's a giant fucking money machine. It operates day and night and they have each guy doing the work of three. You know why I do drugs? Because I think I'd lose my mind without them."

"Why don't you quit?"

"And do what? Work at fucking McDonalds?"

"Okay. I got that. But what about the working conditions at ADM?"

"It's a fucking mess. Dust everywhere. You breathe this shit in all day. There's no getting around it, even with all the vacuum pumps to contain it."

"No gear?"

"There's masks, but they only do so much. I'm probably going to get lung disease just like my old man. He retired at 55—couldn't run the stairs anymore."

"Lot of stair climbing?"

"A lot. That's all I do all day—up an' down stairs."

Talking with Larry makes me wonder if a lot of drug use stems from boredom.

▥

When I got my bedroll on Friday night, it was missing a pillow. Guess who had control of the block? CO Miles.

"CO, I'm missing a pillow. Can I get one from laundry?"

"Not my job."

This has to be because of my earlier lack of willingness to lock myself in. Like it was an attack on him and now he's returning the favor. I'm taken aback by how petty these guys are. Their "us versus them" mentality really gets tiring after 25 weekends.

"Well, what about making a request of another CO or a trusty?" I push my case one more time. But he's not giving an inch. It's payback time for my comment when I refused to shut my cell door.

He just smiles: "Not my job."

I roll the end of my bedroll into a makeshift pillow and use my other blanket to bolster my head so I don't wake up with a headache. In the morning, another CO is on shift and my pillow arrives forthwith.

▥

Ollie bought the Phillip Hamm Collision Garage from his father about three months ago. It's across the street from Applebee's in Greenport, New York. Ollie has a mortgage to pay his dad, as well as all the other bills that go with running a small business.

Five and a half weeks ago, Ollie received a notice from DSS that he was six payments behind on child support. His kids are all grown and in their twenties, but this notice was to pay a tax warrant. Child support arrears become a debt to the state if they go unpaid too long and are above a certain amount. Where the money goes once it goes into the state coffers, nobody knows, but it's sure not going to the kids.

Ollie brought $850 with him to court and promised another $800 within a couple of weeks. The spring collision season was just getting going and business was looking better. He had eight dented cars on his lot to fix. The DA in charge of the case said "too little, too late—six months in jail." The judge agreed and now here sits Ollie.

Why did he get behind? I ask him.

"Heating bills. A body shop has to be kept a certain temperature for the paint to set, and natural gas is costly in a drafty garage." Ollie's heating bills tripled over the cold winter of 2013-14 and since his kids were grown, he made a choice.

"I figured I pay the utilities and catch up on the child support in the spring. At one point, I was dropping close to $400 a month just on utilities—I couldn't keep up."

"And did your lawyer bring any of this up about the cost of energy, etc?"

"My lawyer hardly opened his mouth. I fired that stupid ass. Now I have a new guy."

"Are you aware that they are not supposed to put you in jail on a civil matter, even if it's child support? That's debtor's prison. It was banned over one hundred years ago!"

"Well, my stupid lawyer didn't know about it."

"The way to deal with it is with a Habeas Corpus. The only way they can put you in jail is if you flat out tell them 'I won't pay.' Then they can hold you in contempt, and use that to jail you. But if you make a good faith effort to pay, and you can't pay due to a change in circumstances—in your case, weather and heating bills—you have to be given more time."

"How do you know this?"

"I learned the hard way. I dealt with these fascist family court judges in Albany about five years ago. I had my Habeas heard in Warren County and was out in 48 hours."

"Do you have the paperwork still?"

"Sure do. You want it?"

"Do I want it? Are you kidding? My business is going to be ruined if I'm in here for six months. I'll lose everything."

"OK. I'll send it to you on Monday. But, just one thing—make sure it's filed in another county with an impartial judge who knows nothing about the case. If you made a good faith effort to pay, and they threw you in jail without a due process hearing, then they have to let you out."

"Really?"

"It worked for me."

Family Court is one of the most draconian courts in New York state. It operates in ways that defy common sense. For example:

- If you get behind in child support, you lose your driving license. Which makes it more difficult to get to work and costs you more to get around.
- If you are forced to drive a car because there is no public transport, which is very often the case, then you have to deal with huge fines for operating as an unlicensed driver. If you are a professional, they also can take away your professional license.
- The contempt power of these family court judges is enormous. And they wield it like the Gestapo. The lawyers are officers of the court first. Their financial situation and status among their peers comes second. And the client comes last.

Fathers have very few rights under this system. The system is designed to pit spouse against spouse with the kids in the middle, while the lawyers get rich.

A more rational system would be to start with court-ordered mediation and try to find solutions by first addressing upsets, before any money and custody stuff. In the current adversarial system the money and custody issues are just stand-ins for the retribution of angry spouses.

Ⅲ

Wayne was taking a shower. One thing you don't do when a guy is in the shower is look at him or talk to him. It's even considered necessary to avert your eyes when you walk past that part of the block. I personally don't see what the big deal is. I mean, we all have the same physical equipment. When I was in school, kids used to shower at the same time after gym.

I'm amazed at the level of homophobia in jail. Once a newbie showered with the curtain open and one of the guys called him a "faggot" and a "queer."

"Chill out, man! He's not making a move on you," I said.

"I don't give a fuck—he ought to have that curtain closed. He better not come near me!"

"Wow. You seem awfully edgy for a guy who seems so tough. You might want to take a look at that."

"What?"

"Like how freaked out you are right now. He did absolutely nothing to you. He probably is just used to taking a shower like that."

"I just don't like that gay shit."

"You better stay out of Greenwich Village and The Castro then!"

"Huh?"

"How about just live and let live. He's not bothering you. Let him be."

"Okay, but he better not pull any of that gay shit on me."

"If he is gay, which I don't think he is, I doubt very much he's going to be making any moves on you."

I see Wayne doing his laundry in the shower and ask him why, since there is a laundry service in the jail. He says: "Wash your T-shirt in the sink and see if it's clean."

I do it as an experiment. The water is a gross deep brown color. And when my washing is done, the T-shirt does not smell rancid anymore.

What I came to learn is that all the laundry is put into webbed bags and thrown into the washer where the clothes have no chance to move around and actually get clean.

The inmates are filling out grievance forms about the laundry because the clothes stink and nothing is really clean.

Wayne has two soapy socks draped over his shoulders. His boxers are rinsed and hanging on the cinder block wall.

"What are you using, soap or shampoo?"

"Shampoo works the best."

He wrings out his socks and places them over the block wall. By this little act, he is a claiming a piece of dignity in a place where the overwhelming message is "you don't matter."

Ⅲ

The Power of Habit by Charles Duhigg is a great book. As I read this book, I thought long and hard about heroin addiction. Heroin addicts have very little choice about whether they use again. It's all controlled by the brain's basal ganglia, which is running the show.

The legal theory goes like this: If you know you have a habit and you are aware of it, you have a duty to change, especially if the habit is illegal. Government loves to play this personal responsibility card rather than regulating in any meaningful way the forces that create such havoc in our society: drugs, alcohol, gambling, prescription drugs, and banks. If you walk through my town, or turn on the radio or the TV, or browse the internet, all you see are ads for every imaginable thing that can make you sick, get you into debt or destroy your life.

Once you understand the brain and how heroin acts upon it, you begin to see that without a rational and well functioning support system, these guys I've been talking to have no chance at a normal life. The cues that bring up addiction—anxiety, stress, boredom, money issues, friends, family stress, peer pressure, etc—can start the addiction loop over again.

According to *The Power of Habit*, a person with a bad habit can be transformed into new keystone habits that leads to shifts powerful enough to flow into other areas of their life. For example, a person focused on exercise, who has committed to a daily jog, will experience spillover benefits in many other areas, such as how they eat and drink, how they rest, the kind of people they'll associate with, and the amount of time they spend sitting on the couch.

The drug companies desperately want to sell meds for such problems,[65] but the results are miserable. These meds do nothing to address the habits that lead to drug abuse, and they also kill off the pleasure centers that lead to sexual satisfaction. Who'd want that?

WEEKEND 26

The guys in E-Block have been dealing with a broken toilet at the end of the block for over a week and they are getting fed up. After numerous complaints when nothing has been done, it finally boils over. They all sign a grievance. Max, the lawyer for E-block, spearheads the initiative. He writes the whole thing up and gets everyone to sign on.

I had noticed a smell on the block when I first got there, but was not sure what it was. I assumed it was the rancid clothing that never gets washed out properly. Then I learned that it was the toilet. It had not been flushing for over a week.

Max says: "The maintenance guy comes into the block with a jug.

I ask him: 'What is that? Acid? enzymatic stuff?'

He ignores me. So I press him. 'Show me the bottle.'

He says, 'No,' and splashes a cup full of it in the bowl.

The water bubbles a little and our noses start to burn.

'Acid,' I say to him. 'That ain't gonna do shit. I worked in plumbing when I was a super in New York City—you're gonna need to snake that drain.'

He just looks at me like a dumb fuck and leaves."

CO Dean comes in with the paperwork, and he's all pissed off. The COs hate dealing with this kind of stuff. "I got your grievance," he says. "I can't do anything about Parole putting you in here for minor offenses, but I can get maintenance over here to snake the drain. You guys okay with that?"

Everyone agrees. They all sign the form. Dean goes to make copies.

I was wondering why I'd woken up with a headache on both Saturday and Sunday morning and felt vaguely headachy all day over the weekend, even though I had a pillow in my bedroom. It was the methane leaking out of the toilet.

Ⅲ

Max is a big man. He stands about six feet tall, weighs 295 pounds, and has an extensive overhang of the greater omentum. He describes himself as a "fat bastard." Max has had gout all of his life. "You know to deal with gout, all you have to do is eat the foods that are low in purines," I tell him.

"What the hell are purines? Speak English! Don't forget I'm a roofer with a 1950s lower east side New York City high school education—which ain't much! Most of what I know I learned from the school of hard knocks."

"Purines are compounds in the DNA of red meat and shellfish. Mostly high purine foods are what you need to avoid."

"Well, I'm not getting much filet mignon or shrimp scampi in here!" He cracks himself up at his own joke.

When I arrived on E-Block, I immediately noticed that Max was walking with a limp. The last time I'd seen him— maybe four or five weeks ago—he was walking fine, and going out in the rec yard for some fresh air.

"What's going on with your leg?"

"Oh, that's a long story. But what the hell, we've got time to kill, right?" He laughs again. "I got the gout really bad about three weeks ago. My foot blows up like a balloon. It's red. It's hot. And it hurts like a motherfucker."

"Did you get treatment?"

"Well, yes and no. That's where the story of the dysfunctional human warehouse comes in."

"What happened?"

"So, I'm getting Allopurinol and Colchizine to deal with the uric acid, but I'm not getting any pain meds or anything to deal with the swelling in my leg. I go to the doctor and he gives me a couple of Tylenol, but that ain't touching this kind of pain.

… At about midnight, the pain goes off the charts. My leg is swollen all the way up to my knee. I can't move my leg, and even the slightest pressure is sending me through the roof. I scream for help. The CO comes in and tells me he can't help me. I ask for the sergeant. Sgt Kelly comes down, and he's no fucking use either."

"The pain is off the charts. I tell them: you've got to get me to the hospital. My leg is swollen and it looks like it might be getting infected or something. Kelly says: 'You're not going to the hospital. And you're not getting anything stronger for pain. We don't give out narcotics.'"

"I say to Kelly: 'You don't give out narcotics? Are you fucking kidding me? What the hell do you think Soboxone is? You're gonna give some heroin junkie narcotics, but me, who has a legit problem, you're gonna let suffer? What kind of a fucking sadist are you?' Kelly walks out. I suffer through the night and get up to piss in the morning, but I can't stand on my leg."

A week earlier Max's wife sent a cane to Hudson to help him walk, but CO Kelly refused to let him have it because "it could be used as a weapon" (Max is a 62-year-old cripple at this point).

"I told that stupid overpaid fuck that the DOC already approved the cane upstate in MacGregor and that he had no right to not let me have it. Kelly's response: 'The cane stays in my office until you really need it.' So I hobble around the block and my leg is excruciating. I mean I can barely get around. My meals have to be brought into my cell and I can't even get into the shower."

"So then what happened?"

"Well, this is where they really fucked up. I see the doctor again and tell him about the swelling around my knee and how

I can't even bend the knee. He examines me. 'Does it hurt here?' He presses on the inside of the knee.

'How about here?' He presses on the knee cap and moves it from side to side.

'How about here?' He presses on the outside of the knee. I jump off my seat!"

"The doctor says to the CO, 'We're gonna need an MRI. He has to go to the hospital.'"

"I tell the CO: 'You thought I was bullshittin' you, right? You see!'"

"The MRI results came back positive for lateral meniscus tear caused by unequal weight bearing on the leg because of the gout and the pain. Now these fuckers have a lawsuit they're gonna have to deal with, and those shitheads Sgt Kelly and Lt Hudson are on the top of my list."

Ⅲ

Rick has four older brothers. They all joined the Hells Angels, and all of them did time upstate for various crimes.

"If you want something in jail," he tells me "you have to work the system or be clever at how to get things in."

"What what exactly are you talking about?"

"Okay. When I was doing time upstate for the gun sale I was allowed 20 packs of cigarettes in my monthly box of stuff sent from home. My wife would always send 23 boxes."

"Why?"

"Well, every time I'd get called down to the commissary officer's room and he'd say: 'Winchester, you're only allowed 20 packs of cigs and your box is overweight. We're gonna have to toss some of this stuff'."

"And did they just toss them?"

"Oh, no. Here's how the game works. I know this guy

smokes Newport Lights. I smoke Marlboro. There are 20 boxes of Marlboro and three packs of Newport Lights: 'Officer I only see 20 boxes of Marlboro.'"

"Officer: 'Let me weigh this box again. Oh, my bad. It looks like you're good to go.'"

"So the Newport Lights disappear and I get the extra coffee and peanut butter in my package."

"I've noticed that inmates are crazy about peanut butter. What's up with that?"

"Let me put it this way—it's a great smuggling device."

"Huh?"

"My brother loved to smoke weed. In jail, the only way to get some is to barter your food or bend over in the shower. And if you know my brother—he has a tattoo on his arm of a skull and crossbones— he ain't bending over for nobody."

"So how does he get his weed?"

"When you pack the peanut butter you add a little something extra. I would open up the jars, break the foil seal very carefully, and take out two tablespoons of peanut butter from the center. I'd carefully crush up an eighth of a bag of weed, put it in a balloon and insert it in the center. You put the peanut butter over it, pop it in the microwave for 15 seconds to smooth everything out so it looks undisturbed and then carefully replace the foil on top with a few beads of crazy glue."

"Wow, I'd have never come up with that."

"It looks like it's never been touched."

Prison contraband is not unusual. According to Rick: "Prison is no different than the outside. You can get whatever you want—you just have to be real smart about it. And I'm no dummy."

All the guys on E Block participate in the late evening snack, except Leland. "You know why I fucking hate that guy?" Rick says to me.

"No."

"Well, apart from not knowing shit and pretending to, he's got money in his commissary account. He never shares a goddamned thing, but he always has his hand out whenever we got something going on."

"I could see how that'd be annoying."

"Yeah, well, I'm not feeding that moron, especially after he spends the whole day yelling and doing stupid shit with those two other knuckleheads." Rick points to the Latino kid and the other white guy sitting with Leland.

"Come on!" Max yells to the others. "Let's get the dinner show on the road before lockdown."

The other guys bring over Ramen noodles, Max opens two bags of tuna, I offer my two slices of bread from the morning meal that I did not eat, and one of the other guys pitches in a pickle. Rick has an allergy to seafood so he sits this one out: "I don't eat any of the shit in this place. It's all soy-based garbage full of estrogens. It gives me acne and if you eat it long enough, it'll probably make your dick fall off."

"Yeah, if they use some beef gristle and mostly soy textured protein, they can call it Beef Goulash." Max has a keen sense of what is going down.

Max takes all the ingredients and mixes the Ramen noodles with hot water in one bowl and the tuna and pickles in another. When the noodles are ready, he sprinkles the MSG seasoning pack over them and mixes the two lots together.

"Voila! Dinner is served!" Max cracks himself up again, and starts slathering the mix onto the half stale bread from breakfast.

"You ain't gonna find this at Tavern on the Green!" We all guffaw in unison.

▥

I was out in the yard when I noticed Reese had his ankle bandaged and was on crutches.

"What happened, dude?"

"Basketball accident. I sprained it bad."

"Did they take an x-ray?"

"Yeah, but doctor said no fracture."

"You have a lot of bruising and swelling. In a week when the swelling goes down, they should x-ray it again cuz the swelling will prevent a stress fracture from being seen on film."

Eric: "You the doctor everyone talkin' 'bout in here?"

"Yes, that'd be me."

I ask Eric: "What's going on with your eye and your speech?"

He has an eyelid that is half closed on his right side, and his speech is slightly slurred because of a slight loss of motor control on his lower lip.

"I had a stroke."

"How?"

"I was partying too hard. Did too much Ecstasy and my blood pressure shot up and I bled into my brain."

"Did you just pass out or what?"

"No, I was fine at the club and then when I woke up the next morning, I was paralyzed. I could open my eyes, but could not move my arms or legs. I just kept yelling until someone came. I was in my house for like two days."

"That's not good."

"You're telling me. When I did finally get to the hospital, the doctor said if it had been a couple of more hours, I'd be gone. My breathing was getting really hard."

"Did they do surgery to release the pressure on the brain?"

"I didn't need surgery. But they did give me lots of serious anti-inflammatory drugs. Prednisone?"

"Prednisone. That's a steroid."

"Yeah, that one. And a bunch of other shit."

"You're lucky you're standing here. Why are you here anyway?"

"Child support arrears."

"You're kidding?"

"I know. Fucked up, right? I was in the hospital for like eight weeks and then I can't work because my arms and legs are all fucked up, but they don't want to know nothing. They gave me six months."

"I'm sorry."

"I know. I asked if it was you because I heard about that Habeas you done for that other dude."

"Yes, I'll send it to you. You just need some time to get yourself together and figure out how you're gonna support your kids."

Eric tells me: "After they fucked with the big fat Jew boy, I spent six thousand hours in that law library up at MacGregor. Just enough to make me dangerous."

"I've read (in Malcolm Gladwell's book *Goliath*) that it takes about ten thousand hours to become competent at something."

"Well, I must know something, because my Habeas over the gun conviction is still alive in Federal court after 68 letters back and forth and the NY AG's office is running out of arguments."

"So how did you do it?"

"Do what?"

"Get so good at law?"

"I'm just a dumb fuck. But I kept reading, reading, and reading, until I managed to figure it out little by little. I had the time because of the gout. They never made me do any work up there so I just spent all my free time in the law library."

"Was it a good law library?"

"Oh yes, way better than the piece of shit they have here.

This one is a joke. All the books are out of date and you can only spend one hour at a time. That's not enough time to get anything done."

"How'd you keep your case going?"

"I told these fuckers I'd sue them for lack of due process if they did not give me more access."

"Why due process?"

"If you're an inmate and you don't have access to the law and you're too poor (like me) to be represented, you are denied due process. Look it up! I told these overpaid warehouse schmucks I'm gonna sue them next if I don't get an answer in federal court. I showed them the time stamp on the paper and then showed them my federal complaint against the jail."

"Nice!"

"You like that, huh? I learned that little ditty in MacGregor. None of these guys wants a lawsuit."

"So who let you go?"

"It was Dean and Miles that stood up for me to the bigwigs up front. I have to hand it to them, they did the right thing."

"So now you've got some skills."

"I'm no lawyer, but I know my way around enough to be dangerous to them and that's just enough to get some respect around here."

Max has been poring over his book for a while.

I ask, "What's that?"

"It's the Hebrew Book Chumhuh (*hum-ush* phonetically), or more correctly, the Pentateuch and Haftorah."

"That's a mouthful. What is that exactly?"

"The first five books of the Bible with a portion of the Torah, the rabbinical commentaries."

"And when I hear you in the morning, what do you pray?"

"I pray the oldest prayer in the world: 'Hear O Israel, The

Lord our God is One God.' Deuteronomy 6:4-9. The Jews call it the Shema."

Our food arrives. I ask Max, "Let's pray the Shema over our food." Max says the prayer in Hebrew: *Shema Yisrael, Adonai Eloheinu, Adonai echad.*

We break the bread. It is my first prayer in Hebrew.

Ⅲ

Rick used to be a long haul trucker, a steel cowboy. He worked for Reese-Bolling Trucking in Germantown, NY. On one of those long-haul trips, while he was carrying palettes of cement, the guy unloading the truck pushed the palette too close to the end of the trailer and it tipped over the edge, dropping hundreds of pounds of cement onto Rick.

"I knew I was hurt but I had no idea how bad. I got back in my truck and drove back to New York. By the time I got to Oklahoma, my legs were numb. When I was in Chicago, I had foot drop. I had to use a baseball bat to drop the clutch and change gears."

"What happened?"

"I didn't know for a few days. I was so fucked up when I got back, I was in and out of consciousness. They did a tap on spinal fluid and it was all cloudy—apparently that's not good. The doctors said it was some kind of miracle that I was able to make it home."

"Did they operate on you?"

"It turned out that the cement crushed a whole bunch of stuff in my back and it took some time for the bone chips to work their way into my spinal cord. There's still shit in there."

"So, what'd they do?"

"The one doctor said my spine looked like a jigsaw puzzle. He didn't know what to do with it so they flew this hotshot spine surgeon in from California to do the procedure. It took 12 hours. They had to cut out big sections of the damaged bone, build a titanium cage around the unstable parts, put artificial discs in there, and then tie the whole thing to rods so I can stand up."

"I bet that cost a pretty penny!"

"Quarter of a million bucks. And the bad news was that Worker's Compensation was giving me all kinds of trouble to get the bills paid and get my unemployment insurance. I went through all the money I had in savings and things were getting pretty tight."

"What ended up happening with the bill?"

"We had to take the insurance company to court. After about ten months, the judge finally ruled on it. He was pissed off too. He held up the stack of diagnostic tests and all the legal papers and said to them: 'This should have been dealt with months ago. Pay the plaintiff back pay $45,000 and his disability payments moving forward.'"

"Well, that worked out."

"I guess. But my back is all fucked up. I'll never walk right again. I'm in constant pain, but I get about $6000 per month for that. No thanks, I'd rather be working and have my health back."

"I understand. I deal with people in pain all day long. None of them would trade their health for money. I'm sorry. How have you dealt with the pain in here?"

"When I came in, they would not give me any of the pain meds. The first three weeks were awful."

"What were you on to deal with the pain?"

"When I left the hospital, I was taking six Oxycontin per day, one 125 mg Phentonyl Patch every three days, and 80cc of morphine."

"That's a lot of meds."

"Yeah, tell me about it. I was a fucking zombie. I had to wean myself off the shit but I felt like crap. I'm wondering why I feel so bad all the time and my brother tells me I'm a junkie. He offers to shoot me up with some of his heroin to feel better.

"Did you?"

"Hell, yes. I felt like shit. The sad part is that when I got to the street, I couldn't really afford the drugs the hospital had me on. The only one who could help me was my dealer."

"I told my brother, I'm not a heroin addict. And you know what he tells me? 'Wake the fuck up! You've been an addict since your accident.'"

"Did you continue?"

"I did it for a while, but I thought, *I don't want to go down that road.* So I go back to the doctor. He gives me Ultram (Tramadol—an opioid analgesic for severe pain)[66] and I just cold-turkeyed off the other shit."

"How hard was that?"

"I puked for a few days and then it was over. The pot helped with the nausea."

"You smoke?"

"Always have. Always will. I'm a pothead. I freely admit it."

"Why do you think they refused to give you the Ultram when you got in here?"

"Security overrules all rational considerations. These idiots just follow the rules and don't give a fuck about reality. They had my medical records—a stack of papers about two-and-a-half feet tall. They knew the kind of pain I was in. Even the doctor and the nurse told them to back off and give me the Tramadol."

"Did they?"

"Fuck no. At one point I said to the Sergeant, 'Who the fuck are you to overrule the doctor? Where did you get your medical degree?'"

"Did that change his mind?"

"No, he just shakes his head. It wasn't until Max here starts helping me with a legal complaint that they began to realize that I wasn't fucking around."

"So what happened then?"

"We worked up grievance after grievance. Three in all. The last one had a legal complaint attached. I got my meds the next day."

"How long did you suffer?"

"I was in extreme pain for three weeks. My leg was on fire."

"Sciatica?"

"Yes, that. I mean I live with pain and numbness in my legs and back all the time, but the Tramadol keeps it to a dull roar."

When I'm talking to Rick later, I ask him, "So what got you in here?"

"A parole violation on a charge I already did time for."

"What was it?"

"My mother-in-law wanted money. She figured she could shake me down after I got the Worker's Comp settlement, and I told her that I needed that money for my wife and kids. So she called the cops on me when I was driving without a license."

"What?! Surely she knew calling the cops was going to violate your parole and send you to jail for six months?"

"She told me she thought I'd just get a ticket."

"Is she stupid or what?"

"She doesn't understand that the police are not our friends. They are the human tools that deliver the people to the law merchant for two purposes: to pay money, or to warehouse the body so they can float bonds against the body and receive interest on it."

"Nice. I never understand how depraved people become when it comes to money. You speak to your mother-in-law now?"

"No. When she comes to visit my kids, I go out in the woods with the dogs."

Ⅲ

Juan grabs me right away when we get outdoor rec. "There's a new snag in my case. It turns out that Del has not pled out to his charges and he's gonna take responsibility for the sale to his girlfriend."

"Is that good for you? How?"

"Yes, because it's the same shit he did with me using me as an agent to make a drug sale for him. Neither of us benefited. We were mules."

"You should talk to him."

I get a strong feeling just then that Del will come over to us. A few minutes pass and sure enough, he stops and addresses me.

"You're the guy who spoke up in church."

"Yeah, that's me." I'm looking at this guy. He's impressive. Big. Black. Super strong. I can't keep my eyes off his pecs. They bulge out of his t-shirt and he's got a Frito Lay tattoo on the edge of the muscle that's poking out of his shirt.

"You want to spin?"

We walk a few steps, then I pipe up: "I think it's Juan you're wanting to talk to. I'll let you guys have some time together." I walk off.

They walk and Juan tries to work out a way to get Del to agree in court or in a statement that Juan was not the salesman for his heroin, but merely transferring the stuff as an agent.

Ⅲ

When I pass out of the jail interlock—sort of like an air lock on a space ship, but for keeping out guns and knives rather than keeping in a breathable atmosphere—I realize I've forgotten a book I loaned to Cooper. The title was *Difficult Conversations.*

I loaned it to Cooper to help him communicate with his wife, but he had finished it and passed it on to Stuart without my knowing it. Which was perfect, because he needed to have a breakthrough with Del about taking some responsibility for the drug sale he'd involved Juan in.

The guard hands me *The Power of Habit* through the teller window.

"That's the wrong book," I say.

"You'll probably never see it again. It's being passed around."

"That's okay. I've read it. They need it more than I do. It's a gift then."

"Hey Arnell! This is my last supper. I get steak and eggs or something, right?"

"In your dreams, Doc. It's the same slop-on shit tonight."

"Okay. Thanks anyway for bringing our meals."

"You got it. We gonna miss you around here."

Ⅲ

Sunday evening, May 18th 2014. I pass through the doors of the Columbia County Jail for the last time. Phoenix is waiting to pick me up. She is parked at the end of the visitor waiting area.

The sun is still out. It's warm and the grass is high, still unmowed following the rain. I kick off my Crocs and run through the grass. When I get to the end, I do a little end-zone dance.

Phoenix comes out and we hug. "You're free, honey!"

It's finally over.

EPILOGUE

In one of our conversations as we walked round the yard, Max said: "Given the lack of burning bushes in modern life, how can we know the voice of God?"

When I first went into the county jail, I was angry. I had stood up for what I believed in, and now I had been sent to this alien place with its arbitrary cruelty. At first I was a clod of self-concerns focused mainly on what was happening to me. But gradually as I gained confidence, I found I could listen. As time went on, I listened from nothing, meaning listening in a way where one adds nothing, and leaves aside judgments, preconceived ideas, past experiences, opinions, and assessments. I listened to the life stories of men who had been cast aside.

As a Quaker, I'd had some training in this. For many years, I'd sat in quiet expectant waiting in the Quaker Meeting, when you sit in silence with others in a quiet room. At first my mind-chatter took up all the space. But after some time, it became possible to shut this noise off, and get to nothing. An empty room, a clearing.

Quakers tell of "the persistent voice," a spiritual light inside a person. In the Quaker Meeting, members are led to share that voice. The inner light is in all human beings, and can be recognizable by others who are watching or listening for it.

When I walked out of the Columbia County Jail that Sunday, May 18th 2014, I was a changed man. Over the 26 weekends, I had learned to listen not just to the human suffering, but through it to the compassion and empathy on the other side. I witnessed how the inner light shone in different people in myriad ways, even in people who society considered throwaways. As such, my perception of human beings has been forever altered.

The question I am often asked is, "Was it worth it?" My response is that you can't answer a moral question—a spiritual question—with a pros and cons calculation based on money, status, or comfort. The choice not to pay taxes and withdraw my money from the war system came from a spiritual place. Whether it was worth it didn't really apply because it was a choice made beyond fear.

Jail taught me to support other people and put my selfish concerns aside. I am now able to say to Max: "The burning bushes are not gone. They are just a little harder to find. They have been replaced by a persistent inner voice, a community that listens for that voice with you."

Acknowledgements

My grateful thanks to the Old Chatham Quaker Meeting for support during the most challenging parts of my peace witness with a Clearness Committee, to Don and Merry Lathrop for their generous support of both myself and the book, and to Phoenix Grace, who assisted me with her care, listening and emotional support all through the 26 weekends.

I'd also like to thank Robert Berold and Mindy Stanford, my editors, who thoughtfully guided the book to completion, and Jessica Powers at Catalyst Press for getting it into print.

ENDNOTES

1 Stephen A Stansfeld, Mark P Matheson. "Noise pollution: non-auditory effects on health." *British Medical Bulletin*, Volume 68, Issue 1, December 2003, Pages 243–257, https://doi.org/10.1093/bmb/ldg033

2 Gene Healy: *Go Directly To Jail: The Criminalization of Almost Everything* (Cato Institute, 2004)

3 The Pope's full speech:

No" to an economy of exclusion –

Just as the commandment "Thou shalt not kill" sets a clear limit in order to safeguard the value of human life, today we also have to say "thou shalt not" to an economy of exclusion and inequality. Such an economy kills. How can it be that it is not a news item when an elderly homeless person dies of exposure, but it is news when the stock market loses two points? This is a case of exclusion. Can we continue to stand by when food is thrown away while people are starving? This is a case of inequality. Today everything comes under the laws of competition and the survival of the fittest, where the powerful feed upon the powerless. As a consequence, masses of people find themselves excluded and marginalized: without work, without possibilities, without any means of escape.

Human beings are themselves considered consumer goods to be used and then discarded. We have created a "throw away" culture which is now spreading. It is no longer simply about exploitation and oppression, but something new. Exclusion ultimately has to do with what it means to be a part of the society in which we live; those excluded are no longer society's underside or its fringes or its disenfranchised: they are no longer even a part of it. The excluded are not the "exploited" but the outcasts, the "leftovers".

In this context, some people continue to defend trickle-down theories which assume that economic growth, encouraged by a free market, will inevitably succeed in bringing about greater justice and inclusiveness in the world. This opinion, which has never been confirmed by the facts, expresses a crude and naïve trust in the goodness of those wielding economic power and in the sacralized workings of the prevailing economic system. Meanwhile, the excluded are still waiting. To sustain a lifestyle which excludes others, or to sustain enthusiasm for that selfish ideal, a globalization of indifference has developed. Almost without being aware of it, we end up being incapable of feeling compassion at the outcry of the poor, weeping for other people's pain, and feeling a need to help them, as though all this were someone else's responsibility and not our own. The culture of prosperity deadens us; we are thrilled if the market offers us something new to purchase. In the meantime all those lives stunted for lack of opportunity seem a mere spectacle; they fail to move us.

"No" to the new idolatry of money –

One cause of this situation is found in our relationship with money, since we calmly accept its dominion over ourselves and our societies. The current financial crisis can make us overlook the fact that it originated in a profound human crisis: the denial of the primacy of the human person! We have created new idols. The worship of the ancient golden calf (cf. Ex 32:1-35) has returned in a new and ruthless guise in the idolatry of money and the dictatorship of an impersonal economy lacking a truly human purpose. The worldwide crisis affecting finance and the economy lays bare their imbalances and, above all, their lack of real concern for human beings; man is reduced to one of his needs alone: consumption.

While the earnings of a minority are growing exponentially, so too is the gap separating the majority from the prosperity enjoyed by those happy few. This imbalance is the result of ideologies which defend the absolute autonomy of the marketplace and financial speculation. Consequently, they reject the right of states, charged with vigilance for the common good, to exercise any form of control. A new tyranny is thus born, invisible and often virtual, which unilaterally and relentlessly imposes its own laws and rules. Debt and the accumulation of interest also make it difficult for countries to realize the potential of their own economies and keep citizens from enjoying their real purchasing power. To all this we can add widespread corruption and self-serving tax evasion, which have taken on worldwide dimensions. The thirst for power and possessions knows no limits. In this system, which tends to devour everything which stands in the way of increased profits, whatever is fragile, like the environment, is defenseless before the interests of a deified market, which become the only rule.

4 "Populations in the United States, 2013," article by Lauren E. Glaze and Danielle Kaeble, in *Bureau of Justice Statistics Bulletin*, December 2014, NCJ 248479

5 Information from online source: https://www.cbpp.org/research/poverty-and-inequality/a-guide-to-statistics-on-historical-trends-in-income-inequality

6 For a more detailed look at income distribution in America see the film *Inequality for All*, a documentary that follows former US Labor Secretary Robert Reich as he looks to raise awareness of the country's widening economic gap. Director: Jacob Kornbluth. 2013. http://www.imdb.com/title/tt2215151/

7 *College for Convicts: The Case for Higher Education in American Prisons* by Christopher Zoukis (McFarland & Co., 2014)

8 Information taken from the NPR radio program *Fresh Air* hosted by Terry Gross: "Could Prescription Heroin and Safe Injection Sites Slow the Opioid Crisis?" January 8, 2018. https://www.npr.org/2018/01/08/576457029/could-prescription-heroin-and-safe-injection-sites-slow-the-opioid-crisis

9 Cannabis became legal in New York State for medical purposes when the Medical Cannabis Program was implemented in 2016. Adult-Use (also known as recreational) Cannabis was legalized

in New York State when the Marihuana Regulation & Taxation Act (MRTA) was signed on March 31, 2021. https://www.health.ny.gov/community/cannabis/

10 *Four Decades and Counting: The Continued Failure of the War on Drugs*, by Christopher J. Coyne and Abigail R. Hall. April 12, 2017. https://www.cato.org/publications/policy-analysis/four-decades-counting-continued-failure-war-drugs

11 Quaker considerations on drug addiction:

In AA, alcoholism is considered a spiritual disease. No addict left addiction by themselves. It takes intervention on many levels, physical, spiritual, and community.

As a nation, we tend to want to cover up problems instead of dealing with them. That's why we consume 80 percent of all the prescription medications in the world and illegal drugs are not far behind. (Jeb Bush says Americans consume vast majority of addictive painkillers. http://www.politifact.com/new-hampshire/statements/2016/feb/04/jeb-bush/jeb-bush-says-americans-consume-vast-majority-addi/)

The Quakers have a practice for dealing with life challenges, with the acronym SPICE: Simplicity, Peace, Integrity, Community, and Equality. Sometimes it is SPICES with the extra S referring to Service. Each aspect of this acronym can be thought of as an entry point into spiritual practice. There is no particular order. No single aspect more important than another:

Simplicity means do not be too enamored by things of the world. A house is useful, but a 5000 sq. ft. McMansion is unnecessary. Quakers in the past have been mindful not to put too much attention on making money and acquiring the things money can buy because it pulls attention away from spiritual matters.

Peace is a big part of Quaker life. It forms the basis of getting connected to the inner light, but also forms the basis of honoring the inner light in others. Peace in ourselves is the foundation of peace in the family, the community and ultimately among nations.

Integrity can be looked at two ways. It could be construed as strictly formulaic; that is, adhering to the word of God. Or, it can be a way to honor the voice of the spirit. To listen to the word of the Lord as it comes through from divinely inspired thought, and keep integrity to that. Honoring Word As Self.

Community is the great reservoir of spirit. Without community to hold the space of belonging and the space of spirituality, we are like ships unmoored and adrift at sea. "Whenever two or more are gathered in His name, there is love." Christ gathered his apostles around him because the flame of love burns brighter in community.

Equality. We are one. No one is more valuable than another. We can all share what we have to give. We are now a society of "haves" and "have nots" because the 1 percent seem to think they have some special attribute that gives them the right to manipulate, control, and decide what is best for the other 99 percent. This is not to say that people should not be rewarded for hard work and thrift. The fruits of one's labor are important, but so is a level playing field.

12 Susan Cain's article "The Introvert's Manifesto" appears as a chapter in *Quiet: The Power of Introverts in a World that Can't Stop Talking* (Penguin Random House, 2013). It can be accessed online at: https://www.quietrev.com/wp-content/uploads/2015/05/QR_ebookMay8-2015.pdf

13 Rembrandt: *The Anatomy Lesson of Nicholas Tulp.* 1603. Rijksmuseum Amsterdam, The Netherlands

14 I see the signs of this domination and control returning to America. Racism is creeping back into the culture with things like the Supreme Court striking down parts of the Voting Rights Act and allowing states to put rules in place (voter I.D. cards and narrow poll times) that make it harder to vote if you're poor or Black. While these things worry me, there are much greater changes afoot that are far more sinister.

Martin Luther King talked about the three scourges: racism, militarism, and poverty. While the civil rights movement did address some of the more egregious aspects of racism, this trifecta of social ills is still very much with us in new and different forms. An example is the Total Information Awareness Campaign started by John Ashcroft in the first Bush administration and which has continued apace until its present incarnation under the NSA. The government uses the argument: "If you're not doing anything illegal, then you've got nothing to worry about." But here's the catch—in an age where there is no privacy, people (bright, talented, and also flawed people) will pull back and not step up to make a difference when they know all the details of their lives will be used against them.

In the movie *The Lives of Others*, an upstanding East German playwright decides to write a letter to Der Speigel, a West German newspaper, to expose the high level of suicide in the East German Republic. He quickly becomes a suspect and a tiny little fact about his girlfriend unravels his entire life. She is addicted to medication to deal with her anxiety, and this piece of information is used to manipulate her to get to him.

Our federal government wants all medical records to be electronic. Why? They say for convenience, for ease of treatment, and for cost containment. But, what can happen to people when their medical records become an open book? In a society where there is no more privacy of personal information, where nothing is sacred between a man and woman, between family members, between doctor and patient, or between client and lawyer, everyone can become a target of manipulation and extortion.

15 Many of the same questions that prominent whistleblowers thought about are also central to my Quaker Witness. For a long time our country has unconsciously walked into darkness. The time has come to wake up from the American dream, shake off the stupor of sleep, and walk back into the light.

How do we make peace ideas possible? For starters, we need to examine the worn out notion that war is a solution to problems. The myth of redemptive war must be examined closely for what it is—a sham. Underneath it lies a basic contempt for human life. It believes that in order to create something new, there first needs to be massive destruction. This is not our creation myth. Genesis reminds us that out of the void, God created with word.

16 https://peacetaxfund.org/

Legislation to establish a Peace Tax Fund has been proposed in Congress since 1972, sponsored most recently by Representative James P. McGovern in 2023. Its purpose would be to amend the Internal Revenue Code to allow a conscientious objector to have his or her income, estate, and gift tax payments spent for non-military purposes only.

If ever enacted, the peace tax fund legislation would direct the US Treasury to establish a Religious Freedom Peace Tax Fund for the deposit of income, gift, and estate taxes paid by or on behalf of taxpayers: (1) who are designated conscientious objectors opposed to participation in war in any form based upon their sincerely held moral, ethical, or religious beliefs or training (within the meaning of the Military Selective Service Act); and (2) who have certified their beliefs in writing. The privacy of individuals contributing to the Fund would be protected.

The Peace Tax Fund runs an ongoing campaign for the legislation on behalf of citizens who want the right to pay 100% of their taxes without violating their religious or ethical teachings. Voluntary contributions from some 2,000 individuals and from organizations support the campaign.

17 Rumi, Jalaluddin. "The Fragile Vial" translated by Coleman Barks in *The Essential Rumi*. Harper One (2004)

18 Fifth edition of *The Diagnosis & Statistical Manual*. The DSM, published by the American Psychiatric Association, is the standard reference book used by mental health professionals for diagnosing

and classifying psychological and brain-related conditions.

19 The brains of people who use heroin are not the same as other brains. MRI scans have shown that the Nucleus Accumbens gets forever altered with the use of heroin. This is the part of the brain that registers pleasure. However the brain also exhibits neuroplasticity, and even though tracks of habit can be deeply burned into the wiring of the brain, new pathways can also be created. http://www.psychologytoday.com/blog/ending-addiction-good/201302/neuroplasticity-and-addiction-recovery

20 In 1925, the Supreme Court decided in Linder v US that narcotics addiction is a disease. However, decades later, the courts still make few distinctions between personal responsibility (the subject's ability to control their behavior) and underlying causes of criminal conduct (which include the effects of drugs on personal capacity). But defining drug addiction as a disease is not much of a legal defense because "being in the grip of a disease" is not considered the same as "being under the influence of a drug." One is considered a health issue, the other a crime.

21 "Marijuana may hurt the developing teen brain." http://www.npr.org/blogs/health/2014/02/25/282631913/marijuana-may-hurt-the-developing-teen-brain

22 "Deadly Epidemic: Prescription Drug Overdoses." http://www.usatoday.com/story/money/business/2013/07/28/deadly-epidemic-prescription-drug-overdoses/2584117/

23 "How a big drug company inadvertently got americans hooked on heroin." http://www.huffingtonpost.com/2014/02/24/heroin-epidemic_n_4790898.html

24 Critics question FDA approval of Zohydro. http://www.npr.org/2014/02/26/282836473/critics-question-fdas-approval-of-zohydro

25 "US Government signs off on study using marijuana in treatment of veterans' PTSD." *Wall Street Journal*, March 18, 2014

26 "Why can't we talk about injustice?" Bryan Stevenson on

TED Radio Hour. Monday, March 17, 2014 http://www.npr.org/2014/03/14/288700106/why-cant-we-talk-about-an-injustice

27 "American Gulag: Is the world's toughest regime about to relent?" *The Week*, Aug 14, 2013. http://www.theweek.co.uk/us/54617/american-gulag-worlds-toughest-regime-about-relent

28 TED talk by Daniel Reisel: "The Neuroscience of Restorative Justice." March 2014 https://www.ted.com/talks/daniel_reisel_the_neuroscience_of_restorative_justice

29 "Homeless veteran 'basically baked to death' at Rikers Island while being held on trespassing charge." *NY Daily News* March 19, 2014. http://www.nydailynews.com/new-york/inmate-rikers-island-basically-baked-death-100-degree-room-report-article-1.1726713

30 Pro Persona: Representing oneself, acting as your own lawyer, colloquially "a jailhouse lawyer". If someone is doing his own legal research and schooling himself in the law, he's not forced to take a plea.

31 "Criminologist says antisocial behavior is biological." *NPR Fresh Air April* 30, 2013. http://www.npr.org/2014/03/21/292375166/criminologist-believes-violent-behavior-is-biological

32 "Veterans Courts." *DAV Magazine* March 2014. http://www.dav.org/learn-more/news/2014/veterans-courts/

33 "Amicus Brief for Cameron Douglas." http://www.drugpolicy.org/resource/brief-amici-curiae-support-appellant-cameron-douglas

34 Pema Chödrön: 'There is nobody on the planet, neither those whom we see as the oppressed nor those whom we see as the oppressor, who doesn't have what it takes to wake up. We all need support and encouragement to be aware of what we think, what we say, and what we do. Notice your opinions. If you find yourself becoming aggressive about your opinions, notice that. If you find yourself being non aggressive, notice that. Cultivating a mind that does not grasp at right and wrong, you will find a fresh state of being."

35 "Stand your ground laws." *ProPublica.* March 2012. http://www.propublica.org/article/the-23-states-that-have-sweeping-self-defense-laws-just-like-floridas

36 "Relapse rates for drug addiction similar to other chronic illnesses." http://www.drugabuse.gov/publications/addiction-science/relapse/relapse-rates-drug-addiction-are-similar-to-those-other-well-characterized-chronic-ill

37 M Gossop, L Green, G Phillips and B Bradley. "Lapse, relapse and survival among opiate addicts after treatment. A prospective follow-up study." *The British Journal of Psychiatry* 1989 154: 348–353

http://en.wikipedia.org/wiki/Citizens_United_v._Federal_Election_Commission

http://en.wikipedia.org/wiki/McCutcheon_v._Federal_Election_Commission

38 http://articles.mercola.com/sites/articles/archive/2005/08/13/secrets-of-the-fda-revealed-by-top-insider-doctor.aspx

39 "Federal judge: Gov. Deval Patrick 'is out of line' in banning opioid drug Zohydro." http://www.masslive.com/politics/index.ssf/2014/04/federal_judge_gov_deval_patric.html

40 *Inequality for All.* A film by Robert Reich.

See also the Robert Reich interview with Bill Moyers: http://www.youtube.com/watch?v=q-rpkZe2OEo

41 Tefillin are two small leather boxes attached to leather straps, containing four sections of the Torah inscribed on parchment. Both are attached to the body with straps, one to the heart and the other to the head.

42 CBS *60 Minutes* http://www.cbsnews.com/news/is-the-us-stock-market-rigged/http://www.policymic.com/articles/87719/princeton-concludes-what-kind-of-government-america-really-has-and-it-s-not-a-democracy?utm_source=policymicFB&utm_medium=main&utm_campaign=social

43 See for example *The Fourth Scenario* by Jac Hielema (Santasado,

The Netherlands, 2023)

44 A PINS (Person in Need of Supervision) petition is a written request, often filed by parents, asking the Family Court to get involved when other efforts to control a child have failed.

45 http://en.wikipedia.org/wiki/T%C3%BApac_Amaru

46 For the lyrics of *White Man'z World*, see https://genius.com/2pac-white-manz-world-lyrics

47 See https://www.azlyrics.com/lyrics/notoriousbig/readytodie.html

48 Mark 16:1–8

But when they looked up, they saw that the stone, which was very large, had been rolled away. As they entered the tomb, they saw a young man dressed in a white robe sitting on the right side, and they were alarmed.

"Don't be alarmed," he said. "You are looking for Jesus the Nazarene, who was crucified. He has risen! He is not here. See the place where they laid him. But go, tell his disciples and Peter, 'He is going ahead of you into Galilee. There you will see him, just as he told you.'"

49 "Dangers of Nitrous Oxide." http://www.justsayn2o.com/nitrous.dangers.html

50 "LA County cracks down on laughing gas." https://www.youtube.com/watch?v=hRyDb1DDDQ

51 "Long Term Effects of MDMA." http://en.wikipedia.org/wiki/MDMA#Long-term_effects_on_serotonin_and_dopamine

52 "Neurotoxicity of MDMA." http://www.ncbi.nlm.nih.gov/pubmed/20420572

53 Singh Y.N. "Effects of kava on neuromuscular transmission and muscle contractility." *J Ethnopharmacol.* 1983 May; 7(3): 267–76. Online at pubmed.com. http://www.ncbi.nlm.nih.gov/pubmed/6308355

54 Lehrl S. "Clinical efficacy of kava extract WS 1490 in sleep disturbances associated with anxiety disorders. Results of a

multicenter, randomized, placebo-controlled, double-blind clinical trial." *J Affect Disord.* 2004 Feb;78(2):101–10. Online at PubMed. http://www.ncbi.nlm.nih.gov/pubmed/14706720

55 Lou Reed *Perfect Day.* https://www.youtube.com/watch?v=pgviDNeXQ2w

56 https://genius.com/Lou-reed-perfect-day-lyrics

57 http://en.wikipedia.org/wiki/Eastern_State_Penitentiary

58 "Eleven Worst Foods." http://www.diet.st/11-worst-foods-you-can-eat/

59 "FORENSIC FAILS: Forget CSI—What's happening in America's crime labs is a complete disaster." http://www.businessinsider.com.au/forensic-csi-crime-labs-disaster-2014-4

60 "Lynne Stewart & her not-so-free 'Get out of jail' card." http://jpstillwater.blogspot.com/2014/05/lynne-stewart-her-not-so-free-get-out.html

61 "Prison hinders Lynne Stewart's cancer care." http://socialistaction.org/2013/02/prison-hinders-cancer-care-for-lynne-stewart/

62 "Study: The U.S. is an Oligarchy". http://gawker.com/study-the-u-s-is-an-oligarchy-1563363760

63 http://en.wikipedia.org/wiki/Archer_Daniels_Midland. ADM has been prosecuted for price fixing and violation of the Foreign Corrupt Practices Act (Bribing Public Officials)

64 http://www.imdb.com/title/tt1130080/ Film with Matt Damon *The Informant*

65 "Alcoholism drugs work in study that may dispel doubts." http://mobile.businessweek.com/news/2014-05-13/alcoholism-drugs-work-in-study-that-may-dispel-physician-doubts

66 http://en.wikipedia.org/wiki/Tramadol

Joseph Olejak is a Quaker, a qualified chiropractor, and a member of the Old Chatham Quaker Meeting, where he is clerk of the Peace, Justice and Outreach committee. He is committed to advancing peace and justice through non-violent activism, and engaged in community building and supporting local resiliency initiatives. He lives in Columbia County, New York.

www.ingramcontent.com/pod-product-compliance
Lightning Source LLC
LaVergne TN
LVHW091050080826
845145LV00002B/697

* 9 7 8 1 9 6 3 5 1 1 4 5 1 *